Requisite
for
Revival

Dr. Carl W. Garrett

Trilogy Christian Publishers
A Wholly Owned Subsidary of Trinity Broadcasting Network
2442 Michelle Drive
Tustin, CA 92780
For information, address Trilogy Christian Publishing
Rights Department, 2442 Michelle Drive, Tustin, Ca 92780.
Trilogy Christian Publishing/ TBN and colophon are trademarks
of Trinity Broadcasting Network.
For information about special discounts for bulk purchases,
please contact Trilogy Christian Publishing.
Manufactured in the United States of America

10 9 8 7 6 5 4 3 2 1
Library of Congress Cataloging-in-Publication Data is available.
ISBN 978-1-64773-402-2
ISBN 978-1-64773-403-9 (ebook)

DEDICATION

This work is dedicated with deepest love and appreciation to Frances; my wonderful wife and partner in ministry. To my special daughters Carla and Angela and granddaughters Emory, Ellis, Marley, Sophia, and Sylvia.

ACKNOWLEDGEMENTS

My deepest thanks to Penny Lovell without whose technical skill and assistance this project would never have been completed. To Andrew Justesen whose printing knowledge prepared the project for the first step in publishing.

Special thanks to my dear friend Ron Hale whose help in the initial writing was invaluable; to Dr. Alan Branch for graciously writing the foreword; and to Tresa Mote, my partner in ministry with the wonderful people of Rutlader Outpost Cowboy Church.

Some quotes appear in this manuscript for which no acknowledgement is given. I found these quotes without names on old sermons, in my Bible margins, or on pieces of scrap paper stuck in a file. Thank you to those unknowns who made a contribution to this manuscript.

IN MEMORY OF

Rev. Whitley Garrett, my earthly father and father in the ministry. He modeled for me what a pastor, husband, and father should be. Wilma Garrett, a wonderful mother and an example for both Frances and me in the role of mother, mother-in-law, pastor's wife, and helper.

ENDORSEMENTS

This book addresses the most urgent needs of today's churches and provides guidance in bringing revival to our faith in obeying God's Word. It gives unique insight into one of the greatest passages and scripture and will be a blessing to all who read and study it.

Lieutenant Colonel Chaplain Bill Crow
U.S. Army Retired

Carl Garrett has a deep love for both the Word of God and the people of God. There's nothing he enjoys more than to share a cup of coffee with a new friend, listen to their heart, then guide them to answers in the Scriptures. So grab your Bible and this book, and enjoy time with Carl as he shares nuggets of truth from his years of studying the Scriptures. I know you will be blessed.

Lora Jones
Inspirational speaker and author of Song of a Wounded
Heart

Carl Garrett's Requisite for Revival sounds a much-needed note in our day of declining Christian influence in America. The place of the Ten Commandments in the bringing of revival cannot be overstated: without the preaching of the Law, there will be no deeply felt need for the forgiveness that comes through faith in Christ. And without an understanding of what true obedience to God is there can be no true holiness of life, which is always the by-product of real, life-altering revival. Thank you, Dr. Garrett, for this tremendous offering!

David M. McAlpin, Ph.D.
Senior Pastor, Emmanuel Baptist Church, Overland
Park, Kansas
Associate Professor of Biblical Interpretation, Midwestern Baptist Theological Seminary

Requisite for Revival, written by Dr. Carl Garrett, is a timely reminder to the United States of our need for revival and spiritual awakening, returning to the God of the Ten Commandments is essential to our future as a people. Dr. Garrett served as a pastor and then as a Pastoral Care Consultant in our state convention for years. Dr. Garrett was blessed to have his wife, Dr. Frances Garrett, ministering with him by working with the pastors' wives during difficult times.

Dr. Robert Mills
Executive Director-Treasurer
Kansas-Nebraska Convention of Southern Baptists

Over sixty years ago, I found, read, and absorbed a book on the Ten Commandments written by Elton Trueblood. It is time for another book that can shake and challenge people as Trueblood's book did me. Carl Garrett has given us such a book.

Ernie Perkins, Th. D., Ed. D., D. Min., Ph. D.
Evangelist

Dr. Garrett brings a rich history of decades serving as a pastor in a variety of settings from rural to suburban to his writing. His experience in helping people align their sinful realities with God's unchanging standards in the Ten Commandments uniquely qualifies his perspective of our worldwide need for revival now. The "recipe" is timeless.

Dr. Don Reed

Retired Executive Director of Missions
Kansas City Kansas Baptist Association

Dr. Garrett has many of the same concerns I have for our country. We have tried so hard to take God out of our country. And it has got to stop! Through the Ten Commandments, he wisely reminds us these are not ten suggestions or ten good ideas, but ten ways to show the world we love Jesus.

Rev. Jan Smith

Pastor - Elm Grove Baptist Church
Paola KS

Carl Garrett, a pastor with an evangelist's heart, reveals a love for the Lord and effectiveness as a communicator. His family background has equipped him to be a good pulpiteer. Morally clean! Ethically upright! Doctrinally sound! God has used Carl's spiritual pilgrimage to create a grasp of personal renewal, church revival, and national awakening that floats like a butterfly and stings like a bee. It's a championship read.

Dr. T.O. Spicer
Retired Director of Missions
Spring River Baptist Association

TABLE OF CONTENTS

FOREWORD

Galatians 3:24 says, "Therefore, the law has become our tutor [schoolmaster] to lead us to Christ, so that we may be justified by faith" (NASB). Indeed, the Old Testament law, the Ten Commandments, point out our sin problem and bring the sinner to see his or her need for Christ. The Reformers referred to the Ten Commandments as a mirror: Just as a mirror shows our appearance but cannot change how we look, so the Ten Commandments show us our sin and our need for a savior. In God's moral law, He holds a mirror up to fallen humanity and says, look at yourself! You are a mess! In this way, the Ten Commandments drive us to Christ for grace and mercy.

In "Requisite for Revival," Carl Garrett wonderfully presents the Ten Commandments with evangelistic passion. With skill, humor, and passion he shows how each of the Ten Commandments demonstrates our need for a savior and how God desires to save sinners. He also shows Christians how the Ten Commandments give us God's direction for holy living.

In a day and age of moral chaos, it is refreshing to read a clear explanation of the Ten Commandments. Carl Garrett's moral compass points to true north, and he gives a course we can follow. We can follow it because he's following God's Word.

John 10:10
Dr. J. Alan Branch
Professor of Christian Ethics
Midwestern Baptist Theological Seminary

1.

∾

AMERICA IN NEED

Until America rediscovers her God, removes her idols, returns to the seriousness of worship, and restores the sanctity of the home, there cannot be revival in our land. We have entered a new century, a new millennium, but we have done so with the same old need—the need for America to turn to God and experience revival. Does America need revival?

The answer is yes. Perhaps no scripture better characterizes our nation than Judges 17:6, "...Israel had no King, everyone did as he saw fit." God is no longer King in our land. The "me" attitude prevails: "What I want is what I deserve to have, and I will have it regardless of the cost."

In the fifties and early sixties there were sparks of revival. In many churches, two-week revivals were preceded by two or more weeks of cottage prayer meetings in homes of the members, typically held both in the fall and in the spring. Oftentimes, youth-led revivals were held in the summer. The passion that led to the writing of this book came from being a part of what many believed was the beginning of another "great awakening." It sparked for a while and then the flame began to dim, and revival meetings are almost relics of the past.

Instead of revival in America, we have seen the removal of Bible reading and prayer from our public schools, rioting in the streets, rebellion among our youth; responsibility in the home shunned, rampaging drug use and the lack of restraint of immoral behavior. The expectancy of the "Fifties" quickly turned into the cynicism of the "Sixties." Each succeeding decade has brought new depths of degradation. Today, we place great emphasis on the positive; no negatives in our lives. We do not want to be bound by a list of "Thou Shall Nots." Freedom in every aspect of our life is very much in vogue.

We want the freedom to be ourselves; freedom from authority. Often, we want freedom from God's authority. We have turned our backs on moral laws that seem to thwart our fun as we create our own self-styled freedom" (Huffman 10). We are now twenty years into a new millennium with many asking, "Can America survive?"

There is no shortage of surveys that show that America is in desperate need of revival. The good news is that which man so desperately needs, God has amply provided. The remedy for America is revival. The way is clear. During one of the highest times in the life of Israel—the dedication of Solomon's Temple—God took the opportunity to warn the Children of Israel of the dangers of forgetting His laws and following other gods.

In that conversation with His people, God gave them a clear statement of how to bring about revival in their land. In 2 Chronicles 7:14, God said to Israel, "If my people who are called by name will humble themselves and pray and seek my face and turn from their wicked ways, then will I hear from heaven and will heal their land" (KJV).

Because of the timelessness of morality, the Ten Commandments have great importance for each and every generation, and the present generation is no exception. Some things are always wrong or always right because the character of God never changes. The commandments were applicable in Moses' day just as they

21

were in Jesus' day. They stand with equal importance in the Twenty First Century because Hebrews 13:8 tells us, "Jesus Christ is the same yesterday and today and forever." Today, keeping the Ten Commandments is not a sign of the covenant, but keeping God's Holy Law does show that we are serious about obeying God (Peel 29).

The Self Problem

From 2 Chronicles 7:14, we learn that we must first settle the *"self problem."* All problems begin with self, and restoration must start here. God says we must "humble ourselves." Americans do not handle humility very well. There can be no revival until we come to the place of our wills being broken. We must recognize that self is not supreme. That which is right in our sight is not necessarily right.

The story was told of champion boxer Mohammed Ali, who was aboard an airplane that was about to take off, when the flight attendant reminded him to fasten his seat belt. Ali responded brashly, "Superman don't need no seat belt." The stewardess replied, "Superman don't need no airplane, either!" Ali fastened his seat

22

belt (King Duncan 210). Humility does not come easily. Humility is not popular in affluent America. But God says that is what we must have. There must be a humbling of the heart before there can be a healing of the soul.

The Sin Problem

The "*self problem*" leads to the "sin problem." Not only must we eliminate the "self problem" by humbling ourselves, but we must also solve the "sin problem" that exists in our lives. We must measure ourselves against the Ten Commandments; we must recognize our sins and confess them before God. It is difficult to acknowledge and confess our sins, but that is what God says we must do. It is often very easy to see what 2 Chronicles 7:14 calls the "wicked ways" in others, but it is very difficult to acknowledge them in ourselves. We have developed a new vocabulary to keep from calling sin what it really is. We are now "dysfunctional"; we live an "alternative lifestyle"; we have a "significant other," who lives with us, but in America today, we do not sin. Before we can have revival in our land, we must see sin for what it is and personally acknowledge it in our own life.

The Separation Problem

It is this *"sin problem"* that leads to the *"separation problem,"* the separation of man from his Creator. We must surrender ourselves to God. In the words of the chronicler, we must "turn from our wicked ways." The New Testament calls us to repent of our sins. Repentance is a turning away from our own ways. More importantly, repentance involves turning toward the way of God. Vance Havner, a preacher from another age, told the story of a group of small boys who went out to play ball and discovered when they got to the playground that no one had brought a ball. "Forget the ball," one said, "Let's get on with the game" (Hester 186). The church is trying to play without the ball when we try to have revival without repentance. The church can do many things after she repents, but she can do nothing until she repents.

America needing a revival is a given. At the time this book is being put in its final form our nation is in the midst of a major battle with a coronavirus. Scientists are desperately seeking a cure and the nation is in lockdown. Noted evangelists and television pastors are suggesting that this may be God's wake-up call. The question to be answered is *will we humble ourselves, pray, and turn from our wicked ways?* The formula for revival is very clear in God's Word. Many believe we stand on the threshold of a revival. Will we experience one? The jury is still out. There is yet a determination to be made. Let us return again to 2 Chronicles 7:14.

Note that the verse begins with the preposition "if." It is a certainty that God stands willing to send revival. He says, "I will." What is not certain is the *"if" question*. Will we meet the requirements set forth by our Creator? Will we humble ourselves? Will we pray and seek His face? Will we turn from our wicked ways?

A second thing that God says is, "If my people." Please, note what God is saying. He is not waiting upon the lost people to be saved to send revival. He is waiting for the saved people to be revived. First Peter 4:17 tells us that "judgment must begin at the house of God" for America to experience revival. For the churches of America to have revival, the hearts of those who make up the true church must be humble. Each needs to turn from their wicked ways and confess their sin and seek the face of God. It is in the hearts of God's people where the spark of revival will start and hopefully burst into the flame of revival so needed in our land.

25

By looking to the Ten Commandments, we will see how the commandments must become a part of our lives, both individually and corporately, for revival to take place. Revival will not start nationally. It will start in scattered localities. It will not start large. It will start in the life of one here and another there—slowly, revival will spread. You could be one of those from which the spark of revival begins to burst into flame!

When Moses was in the desert tending his sheep, he saw a burning bush and met God in a deeper way. It was that particular bush burning, but it could have been any bush. Are you open to being one of the bushes through which God works? Are you willing to be open to God's will in your life? Are you willing to turn from your ways to His way?

The Psalmist asked, "Will you not revive us again?" (Psalms 85:6). The answer is yes, only if "God's people will humble themselves and pray."

Two revivals I have experienced stand out in my memory. They were not isolated events. They were happening frequently in my teen years and early years of ministry. That I might experience one again is my prayer and part of the reason for the writing of this book.

The first one took place in a small Southwest Oklahoma town where my father was pastor of the First Baptist Church. The church prepared for the revival in a way that was not uncommon at the time. Two weeks of "cottage prayer meetings" were held in individual homes for two weeks preceding the revival. People gathered in homes to pray, and they were specific in their praying. They named names of friends and relatives they wished to see saved.

The revival began on a Sunday morning, and the first week the evangelist primarily preached to the church. He preached that revival must begin in the House of the Lord. He called God's people to the altar for prayer and rededication, and many came.

Two events stand out. We lived in the parsonage next door to the church. My father awakened at 2 in the morning and noticed the lights were on in the church auditorium and there were cars parked in front. He dressed and went to see what was going on. What he found was that several men had felt led by the Lord to come to the church and pray for one man, George. After some time in prayer for George, the men left. As we were sitting at the breakfast table, there was a knock on the kitchen door. An excited deacon came in and said, "Preacher, I just led George to the Lord!"

That same day in a driver's education class, a star athlete turned around in his desk and whispered to me, "Carl, how do I get saved?" I replied, "I will talk with you after class." He wasn't satisfied with that answer, and we got a strong reprimand and a threatened punishment. He was saved that night.

As a result of the revival, the only beer joint in town closed. Other churches in town experienced people coming to the Lord. One hard-nosed man was quoted as saying, "All my friends got saved and joined that [blankety-blank] church"

Could something like that happen again? It can if God's people will commit to the words of 2 Chronicles 7:14.

In the seventies, I preached a number of revivals. God blessed that ministry; one stands out. It was a small town in south central Oklahoma. The pastor had been saved in a revival where my father was pastor. They had prepared well. The pastor told me the week before they were expecting to see God at work. He had no idea what he was going to see!

During that week we saw twenty-one adults come to the Lord. Included in that number was the chairman of deacon's wife and the pastor's nineteen-year-old son. The church had licensed him to preach nine months earlier. He stood before the congregation and said, "You are not going to believe this, but I just got saved. I knew nine months ago when you licensed me that I wasn't saved, but I thought, 'If I will do that God will let me off the hook.'"

Revival, can it happen again? Yes, it can. Revival, does America need one? Yes, it does. Will it happen? Yes, if God's people will heed God's calling. Will we? Since you are reading this book, you are part of the answer.

2.

∽

REDISCOVERING OUR GOD

THE FIRST COMMANDMENT

And God spoke all these words: "I am the Lord your God, who brought you out of Egypt, out of the land of slavery. You shall have no other gods before me."

Exodus 20:1–3

With a finger of fire from a holy cloud from the top of a mountain, Almighty God wrote for man two tablets of law: the Ten Commandments. The first set of laws teaches man how to relate to God—our believing; the second set of laws, teaches us how to relate to one another—our behaving. For millennia, these holy words formed the basis of law and governments. For more than two centuries, these commandments formed not only the basis of the constitution of

31

the United States of America, but they were also the foundation of the morality of our society.

Until 1980, God's holy Laws were generally accepted as the basis of our society. In 1980, the Supreme Court of the United States, in a 5–4 decision, without hearing any oral arguments, ruled in Stone v. Graham that "the school children of Kentucky have the constitutional right not to be assaulted by the presence of the Ten Commandments on their classroom walls." In revealing its rationale for the decision, the court said, in part:

> "If the posted copies of the Ten Commandments are to have any effect at all it will be to induce the school children to read, meditate upon, perhaps to venerate and obey the commandments. However desirable this might be as a matter of private devotion; it is not a permissible state objective under the Establishment Clause."

> "...the passive display of the Ten Commandments was not permitted because some students might obey them" (Hughes 11).

First given to God's people in Exodus, the Ten

Commandments are repeated again in the book of Deuteronomy, because one generation has passed away and the new generation did not know God's holy Law. The 1980 Supreme Court ruling would lead us to believe that the same is true today. Some Americans know the words of the commandments; they just don't know them in practical living. Surprisingly, there are many church people who do not even know the words of the Ten Commandments!

A starting place for revival is found in 2 Chronicles 7:14 where God said "If my people who are called by my name, will humble themselves and pray and seek my face..." If America is to experience revival, Americans must return to the Law of God. In order to return to the Law of God, America must return to the God of the Law—we must seek the face of God. America must "rediscover God."

In Exodus 20:1–3, God begins instructing His people in His ways: "And God spoke all these words: I am the Lord your God, who brought you out of Egypt, out of the land of slavery. You shall have no other gods before me."

Position of this Commandment

The *position of this commandment*—"You shall have no other gods before me"—is of utmost importance. A survey of college students found that 90% of them would re-arrange the Ten Commandments and put the second table of the law, the ones dealing with man's relationship with man, first and the ones dealing with his relationship with God last. This statistic probably best represents the thinking of many Americans today.

It was not by accident or random choice that God gave this commandment as the first. It is first not only in sequence but also in importance. The first Law states "I am the Lord your God..." The starting point of time, religion, and morality is God. The first essential of all true thinking and right living is God. To be wrong here is to be completely wrong. One of the great sins of our country is that so many are so wrong on this point. We have made ourselves many gods. Many Americans have lost a sense of personal walking and talking with God, who birthed our great nation.

When Jesus was asked what the most important commandment is, Mark 12:29–30 records, "'The most important one,' answered Jesus, 'is this: 'Hear, O Israel, the Lord our God, the Lord is one. Love the Lord

your God with all your heart and with all your soul and with all your mind and with all your strength.'"
To fully appreciate the position of the commandment that we are to have no other gods before Him, we must begin to develop an understanding of the person of this commandment.

A college student once said, "God is a little presumptuous, isn't He? What makes Him think He has the right to be number one?" For ages, the answer to that question has been that, at the beginning of the commandments, there is *a personal identification*, not only of the One speaking but of the ones spoken to. "The initial six words, 'I am the Lord your God,' provide a dynamic communication of God's gracious nature. He was I, not it. They were you, not them (Hughes 32). When God delivered His commandments, He took time to preface His remarks with a statement that provides the basis for our obedience. He didn't just authoritatively say, "Here are ten things you shall not do." Instead, He reminded the people that He was a living God, personally concerned for each of them. His initial remark is not a command. His initial remark is the basis on which all the commandments rest. He reminds His people that He is the God who had brought them out of the land of Egypt, out of the house of bondage.

The starting point for obedience is the awareness of God's fatherhood followed by the awareness of our sonship, an awareness of our family relationship (Huffman 25). A simple answer to the student's question as to whether God has the right to presume to be number one would be to respond, "Because of who He is, He can demand what He commands. Because of who we are, His people, we must listen and obey."

Positive Affirmation

Building upon our awareness of whom He is, in the First Commandment we find a *positive affirmation.* "You shall have no other gods before me." The affirmation in the verse is that "The God of the First Commandment is God, there are gods but no other God." In his book on the Ten Commandments, "Liberating Limits," John Huffman says, "...we must make a distinction between God with a capital "G" and god with a small "g". God with a capital "G" is the one who created and sustains us; whereas the god or gods with a small "g" are those that have supreme authority in our lives, those to which we have made our ultimate commitment in life. They need not be the true God" (Huffman 28).

Every time Israel crossed a border into another land during their pilgrimage from Egypt to the Promised Land, they ran into another god. A polytheistic world existed when these commandments were given. It sounded strange to talk about one God when the world was filled with many gods. In religious circles today, it doesn't sound strange to speak of one God, but it is strange. Even among those who profess to be followers of the one true God, many strange gods are found.

God and His Word do not give us the privilege of an argument with God. God and His Word do not give us the privilege of an alternative to God. We need to take a look at one more thought in this commandment and that is the presumption in this command. There are a number of presumptions or assumptions that could be made on the basis of what is said and not said in this commandment. First, *every person has a god*. The First Commandment does not tell us to have a god; it tells us to have the proper God. Man was created to worship God. Inside every human heart, there is a God-shaped vacuum that only the true God can fill.

Unfortunately, man will attempt to fill this vacuum, all too often with false gods, not the true God. The question is not "Do you have a god?" You do! The question you must answer is "Who is or what is your God?"

Secondly, *we will become like our God.* We are told in the Psalms that we become like the god we worship. Our morals reflect the god we worship. It is easy to see what gods America is worshiping by observing the conduct of her people. The god of self has produced a "me" generation. The god of wealth has produced a materialistic society. The Hollywood gods and goddesses of sex and perversion have produced a society that has cast off all restraints. The missing ingredient today—America rediscovering its God—is a result of those who profess to be followers of the God of the First Commandment yet so often have not become like Him. Believing in the true God helps us see that God is different. Our actions and attitudes show the world that we, His people, are different. At one time there was found on the menu of the Paramount Studio restaurant these words: "Cecile B. DeMille says, 'Don't Just Act the Ten Commandments, Live Them!'" (Huffman 22).

A little girl was intently working on a drawing.

When asked by her teacher what she was drawing she responded, "I am drawing a picture of God." The teacher replied, "But nobody knows what God looks like." With the candor that only a child knows, the girl said, "They will when I get finished!" When the people of God begin to live the teachings of God, the world will begin to pay attention to God. The world will begin to know what God looks like! Jesus came to show who God is. He left us to show Him to the world.

Presumption

There is a third *presumption* in the commandment. If you are willing to have no other gods, you can have God. If we will put all other gods out of our lives, God says, "l will show up." Job asked, "Can one by searching find God?" (Job 11:7 KJV). The answer is no. Yet, Jesus in Matthew 11:25 said, "I thank you Father... that you have hid these things from the wise and have revealed them unto babes." We cannot find God on our own, but when we come to the place where we are willing to make Him and Him alone our God, He will find us, then we can know Him. In John 17:3 Jesus said, "And this is life eternal, that they may know you the only true God, and Jesus Christ whom you have sent."

In Exodus 20:2, God says, "I am the Lord your God." He is simply saying, "I can be real, personal to you." It's not enough for you to affirm there is a God. It's not enough for you to say, "He is the God." You need to be able to say, "He is My God." Can you say that? Can you say, "Jesus is my Savior? He is my Lord. He is my God" (Vines 17–18).

Former Russian President Boris Yeltsin once told senior correspondent David Aikman of "Time Magazine" that he was thinking of ways to get priests into the Russian school system to speak on ethics morality. Aikman wrote, "That prompted me to observe that it took the United States 200 years of religious freedom to drive Christianity out of the schools and the Soviet Union 70 years of atheism to bring it back" (Hughes 16).

When an individual or a nation comes to the place where they think they have liberated themselves from outdated divine law, in reality they are committing themselves to supreme bondage. Someone once said, "You cannot break the Ten Commandments; all you do is break yourself against them!" It is only when we act in obedience to the commandments of God, as restricting as they are to some of our animal instincts, that we are truly set free!

Revival must begin at the House of God with God's people. What are we going to do with what we know about this First Commandment? There are at least three possibilities. Some will continue to do just as they have been doing, *simply ignore it,* as if it didn't exist. Some will *deliberately disobey it,* knowing full well the reality of one true God yet they will bow themselves before their own gods, the gods of the world. And *some will obey it.* Will you obey it?

3.

❦

REMOVING THE
IDOLS

THE SECOND COMMANDMENT

You shall not make for yourself an idol in the form of
anything in heaven above or on the earth beneath or
on the waters below. You shall not bow down to them
or worship them; for I, the Lord your God am a jealous
God, punishing the children for the sin of the fathers to
the third and fourth generation of those who hate me,
but showing love to a thousand generations of those
who love me and keep my commandments.

Exodus 20:4–6

The premise upon which we are building as we move through the Ten Commandments as the Requisite for Revival is twofold. The first premise is that America needs a revival. There are few of God's people that would dispute this fact. The second premise is that, if the people of God are to experience the power of God, they must return to the precepts of God; His law.

In the First Commandment, we are told in a straightforward way that we are to worship the right God. In the Second Commandment, we find that we must not worship the right God in the wrong way. If surveys are to be believed, the greatest sin in our land is not that America does not believe in God, it is that we do not worship the God of whom we profess to believe.

In visiting foreign lands, it is a strange feeling to stand and watch people dancing and singing before their hand-fashioned gods or prostrate themselves before a gigantic statue in quiet reverence, as birds sit on the god's head, fly into his eyes and ears, and make their deposits upon him. In the Second Commandment, we are warned against such sacrilege. Most sophisticated twenty-first century Americans would not consider this commandment to be of great concern to them. There are no idols in their homes or lives, and, by their own understanding, they are correct because they have chosen to define the term "idol" rather than be guided by God's definition of the word.

Listen to the words of God as He gave the Second Commandment on the mountain and continues to speak to us through it today.

You shall not make for yourself an idol in the form of anything in Heaven above or in the waters below. You shall not bow down to them or worship them; for I, the Lord your God, am a jealous God, punishing the children for the sins of the father to the third and fourth generation of those that hate me, but showing love to the thousands who love me and keep my commandments.

Exodus 20:4–6

Confuses the Creator with the Created

The person who worships anyone or anything other than the one true God, is *confusing the creator with the created*. In so doing, they tend to magnify their own role. Ancient Israel is a prime example of this. Chosen by God to become a "kingdom of priests and a holy nation" (Exodus 19:5–6), they were to be God's representatives to the whole world (Deuteronomy 7:6-8) and a "light to the nations" (Isaiah 42:6). Sadly, the

45

children of Israel often abandoned their priestly role to "do that which was right in their own sight," following the gods of other nations. The Israelites wanted an earthly king like everyone else; they wanted to control their own destiny.

Ministers and sermons are accepted when talking about the failures of history; however, they are not so popular when applying those examples to daily lives of their listeners. Mankind was created to rule over all creation. That rule was only possible when man was ruled over by the Creator. In our society, Americans want to be in total control. We want God in our lives as long as He doesn't get in the way of our living. Romans 1:25 is a verse that needs to be heard and meditated upon. Paul says, "They exchanged the truth of God for a lie and worshiped and served the created things more than the Creator..."

Magnifies his Role and Minimizes the Requirements of God

By confusing the Creator and the created, man often *magnifies his role and minimizes the requirements of God.* God said, *don't, absolutely do not make any idols. He said, don't worship any idols.* "I am a jealous God," we are told. The word "jealous" often has a very negative connotation, but in this case, jealous is a "grace word." If God were not a jealous God, we would be in bad shape. Because He is a jealous God, He wants nothing less than the best for us. If He were not a jealous God, He would leave us to pursue, without correction, our own way, and "the way of man ends in destruction."

In thinking of the subject "Removing the Idols," remember who the Creator is and who the created is—do not confuse the roles of the two. Failure to remember the Creator leads to choosing the lesser over the greater. Former President Jimmy Carter wrote a book called "Why Not the Best?" When the created one chooses a god of his own making, he is settling for far less than the best. By choosing the lesser over the greater, man loses the genuine for the imitation. Most idol worshipers deny they worship an idol. The idol is just a visible representation of their invisible God.

While Moses was on the mountain receiving the commandments from the hand of God, Israel became afraid because Moses was gone so long. In a sense, even Moses became an idol; he represented God to them and without Moses, the Children of Israel felt lost. So, the Israelites decided to make a god, attempting to fashion a representation of God to keep before them. As soon as they had finished fashioning the statue, Aaron declared a feast to the "One true God," but neither Moses nor God was pleased. In fact, Moses was so displeased that he became the only man to ever break all the commandments at one time! God was so displeased that many of the people died and all of the children of Israel suffered. They had the best; they had God, Himself. He had been with them every step from Egypt and here they were with gods of gold in His place. Gods that are created by the created distort God. They can never show Him as He is. Manmade images of God degrade God. God, who made all that has been made, can never be adequately represented by an image.

The people of Israel professed their innocence by proclaiming they were worshiping the idol because it reminded them of Him. God didn't buy that anymore than your spouse, upon finding you in a romantic embrace with another, would accept your explanation, "Honey, it isn't what it seems. I was just doing that because she reminded me so much of you!"

Abuses the Future for the Present

By choosing the lesser over the greater, man *abuses the future for the present*. The fully expanded commandment says that when man breaks the commandment, the consequences are visited to the third and fourth generation. This is troublesome to many. In fact, it is seen as downright unfair, but it is not. God is not saying it is His will that the children suffer for the sins of the parents. It isn't. He does not want the parents to sin and he does not want the children to suffer but the natural consequences of sin are the fruits they bear. Many of you know firsthand of the hurt experienced because of the sins of your parent.

Ask any child of an alcoholic or the child of one who has committed a crime, about the ridicule and hurt they have gone through. Observe around you the results of living life for one's self and leaving God out. Observe the hurt in the lives of those who have no spiritual training. Talk to a Christian counselor and ask about the hurting children, whose lives are being destroyed because of the sins of their parents. You cannot violate the laws of God without your children hurting. It hurts God that they are hurt. That is why He included these words in the law. If for no other reason, do not do it for the sake of your children. Just don't do it!

Do not bow down to the goddess of sex and have that affair and destroy your marriage. Don't do it for God's sake! Don't do it for your children's sake! Don't do it! Don't bow down to the god of materialism and sacrifice your family for possessions. Don't do it! The futures of so many have been shortchanged for a moment of pleasure here, or a short cut there. "Don't do it!" God says.

Coveting the Sacrilegious Instead of Salvation

The person, who worships anyone or anything other than God, is guilty of *coveting the sacrilegious instead of salvation*. The five most popular gods in today's America are *position, power, possessions, popularity,* and *pleasure*, not necessarily in order of popularity.

Position

Position is a god to many. Titles, stations, parking spots, and choice offices have become the driving obsession in far too many lives. Many find themselves caught up in the quest for position in spite of their efforts to stay above it. Jockeying for position has become a way of life for far too many.

Power

Power is closely related to position, but it moves beyond position to control and authority. Power is not always related to position. Children learn to manipulate their parents through temper tantrums and other behaviors. A flight attendant on an airplane was telling another attendant about a little boy on her plane on a recent flight. She described him as the rudest child with whom she had ever had to deal. "He had the upper hand," was the way she summed it up. The boy's mother had the authority by virtue of her position, but the boy had assumed the power. This happens in many ways.

Possessions

Possessions and wealth control so many. The more possessions we have, the more we want, until nothing satisfies us. Fashionable homes, expensive automobiles, club memberships, and designer clothes consume many Christians. They have a way of becoming more important than God and the church.

Popularity

Popularity, social status, having the right address, belonging to the right club or even the right church is important to so many. If we are not careful, popularity becomes our god and we will do what we know we should not to gain popularity.

Pleasure

Pleasure is the supreme object of worship in America. We bow down to what makes us feel good—"me" first. What gives me pleasure is of utmost importance. The entertainment world would have us bow down to the gods and goddesses of pleasure. Do what turns you on without considering the consequences.

God says, "Don't do it." The reason He says this is that He is a jealous God, who wants nothing but the very best for each one of us. Instead of coveting the five "P's," we need to place God in the proper position because He alone can give us what we truly need. We

need to look at the *four characteristics of salvation.*
What the world offers us is the opposite of what God
provides for us. The world offers that which is im-
perfect. God provides us with *perfect* salvation. In
2 Corinthians 5:21, it reads, "God made him who had
no sin to be sin for us, so that in him we might be the
righteousness of God." The world would have us think
that it cares, but the world is really impersonal. God
provides *personal* salvation. John 3:16 tells us, "For
God so loved the world that He gave His one and only
son, that whoever believes in Him shall not perish but
have everlasting life." The gods of the world are im-
potent, while God is all *powerful.* In Romans 5:9, we
read, "Since we have now been justified by his blood,
how much more shall we be saved from God's wrath
through him!" Things of the world are temporary,
whereas God provides that which is *permanent.* Hebrews 7:24 reads, "but because Jesus lives forever, he
has a permanent priesthood." When God says, "don't,"
He says it because there is a reason. We don't need
an imitation god when we have the real thing. The
following scripture references provide further clarification: Colossians 1:15; Hebrews 1:3; John 14:9.

When the gods of America are sacrificed on the altar before the God of creation, then the creature will bow in humility before his Creator. When the gods of America are sacrificed before the God of creation, then the creature will no longer be afraid to seek the face of his Creator. When the gods of America are sacrificed on the altar before the God of creation, the creature will no longer need to be called to prayer, he cannot be kept from prayerful communication with His creator. When the gods of America are sacrificed on the altar before the God of creation, then the creature will find their wicked ways pale in the allure of their Creator. When the gods of America are sacrificed on the altar before the God of creation, then the creatures will find themselves heard by their Creator. When the gods of America are sacrificed on the altar before the God of creation, the creature will find his sins are forgiven, his land will be healed, and life will be full and meaningful, as God intended. The God of the universe must be rediscovered in our land, and we must rid ourselves of all that competes with Him for first place in our lives.

4.

❧

REFRAINING FROM PROFANING

THE THIRD COMMANDMENT

You shall not misuse the name of the Lord your god, for the Lord will not hold anyone guiltless who misuses his name.

Exodus 20:7

The Ten Commandments are a mighty moral mirror. They reveal something of the character and the heart of God, and they reveal to us the sin in our hearts and lives. This mighty moral mirror reflects our blemishes and badness, but the mirror has no power to remove the blemishes, only the ability to reflect them.

God had a plan. History recorded that plan. God knew that down the road from Mount Sinai stood another mountain, Mount Calvary. God knew that on the other side of the commandments was Christ. The Law could command, but it could not convert. It could challenge us, but never change us. It could point the finger at us, but it could never singlehandedly remove sin from our stony hearts. Most importantly, the Law chases us into the waiting arms of Jesus Christ. Romans 3:20 says that God does not accept people simply because they obey the Law. *No, indeed!* All the Law does is point out our sin.

In other words, we look at the Law and the standards of a Holy God and say to ourselves *there is no way on earth that I can live up to those standards.* We ask, "Dear God in heaven, I need help!" Out of a loving heart, God says to every seeking soul, "Come to me; that's why I am here." Only He has the power to convert and change.

Greg Laurie, in his book entitled "Life, Any Questions?" illustrates this very well through depicting a courtroom drama. Satan is the tall, handsome, confident prosecuting attorney. Jesus serves as the court-appointed attorney. The judge is the Heavenly Father. The person on trial represents any person. For weeks, Satan has pointed out the sins and shortcomings of the person on trial. In his concluding remarks Satan says,

"As we all know this person has broken the law. You have said, 'For whoever keeps the whole law and yet stumbles at just one point is guilty of breaking all of it.'" (James 2:10).

Obviously, this person on trial deserves judgment and death. At last, Satan sits down with a smug and contented look on his face, knowing that he has nailed the defendant to the wall.

The Defense Attorney stands up and asks the Judge, "Permission to approach the bench?" Jesus then walks slowly, leans forward, and with His first word changes the whole outlook on the proceedings. He says to the judge, "Father, we both know this person has done everything the Devil has said. But we also know that You sent Your son to pay the penalty for that sin, so I ask You to forgive this client on my behalf." "You're right," says the Judge. With that, the Judge looks at Satan and says, "Case dismissed. All is forgiven." The judge pounds his gavel, emphasizing the finality of that statement.

Trying to live up to the standards of the Law (in your strength and power) without the grace of God and the guardianship of Jesus, you will fail miserably in pleading your case before the judgment seat of God in the courtroom of eternity. There is one Lawgiver. There is one Lifesaver. There is only one lifeline thrown from a Holy God to a sinful world. When a repentant person grabs that lifeline causing grace to open the floodgates of forgiveness, that person becomes a child of God. Then and only then does the Heavenly Father's name become so very important. The child of God will—should—refrain from the profane use of God's high and holy name.

The Third Commandment speaks of this. Listen to God's Law concerning the use of His name:

> *"You shall not misuse the name of the Lord Your God for the Lord will not hold anyone guiltless who misuses his name." Or as the familiar King James Version says, "Thou shalt not take the name of the Lord thy God in vain"*

(Exodus 20:7).

Ingredients of a Name

If America is to experience revival, there must exist a holy reverence for the name of God, a refraining from profaning. As we consider refraining from profaning, we need to first consider the ingredients of a name. It is interesting to hear young parents talk about the names being considered for a baby on the way. The list of possible names is endless. A final choice of names that combines the names of two special people becomes a name with a special meaning. It is common to hear a child saying, "Someone called me a name!" Oftentimes the name is not bad, it just is not the child's name and the child does not like it. For many reasons, names are important. In reference to the name of the Lord, there are three important ingredients.

Reputation

The first ingredient of a name speaks of the *reputation* that person bears. The book of Proverbs has much to say about the importance and impeccability of a good name. Proverbs 22:1 says, "A good name is more desirable than great riches; to be esteemed is better than silver or gold." We have been eyewitnesses to the defamation of a name as the world watched Richard Jewell go from a hero to a media-proclaimed bomber. In an interview, he was asked about the monetary settlement he had arrived at with one of the networks. His reply: "The money is not what I am after. All I want is to get back my good name and reputation." In many ways, it will never happen. Forever, Jewell's name will be linked as a suspect in the 1996 Atlanta Olympic bombing tragedy.

There are some names that you cannot hear without negative feelings being generated. How many children have you known named Judas or Jezebel? Most of us have heard the phrase or perhaps said, "Don't ever mention that name around me."

Respectability

The second ingredient of one's name speaks of *respectability* or power. Oftentimes we will hear one child admonishing a younger sibling to do something and when told they are not going to do it, they will back it up with power words, "Dad told me to tell you." The word "Dad" carries special power. "The boss said"; "the IRS said"; "the doctor said."

A story is told of the young Duke of Kent and the young Prince of Wales. While playing one day, they observed a young cockney boy hiding behind a stone wall deftly throwing rocks and knocking off the tall hats of the British Bobbies as they walked by on the other side of the fence. Now, the two royal siblings knew better, but this looked like fun, and they entered into the rock throwing. They were so engrossed in their mischief that they failed to see the big policeman slip up behind them. Suddenly, they were swept up in his powerful arms. The policeman asked the first boy, "What is your name?" Pulling himself up to his full height, the first boy said with dignity, "I, Sir, am the Duke of Kent!" The policemen then turned to the second boy and asked, "Who are you?" With equal royal demeanor, the second youth replied, "I, sir, am the Prince of Wales!" The little cockney boy, not to be outdone, stood to full height and exclaimed, "And I, sir, am the Archbishop of Canterbury!"

Rights

The third ingredient in a name is *rights*. There are certain things that just go with having a certain name. The Duke of Kent and the Prince of Wales had the authority, the right to order the policeman around. Their behavior at the moment may not have shown it, but their names affirmed it. We are told in John 14:13–14, "I will do whatever you ask in my name, so that the Father may be glorified in the Son. You may ask me for anything in my name, and I will do it." That is our right because of the name we have been given, the name of Jesus.

Insights into God's Name

In addition, we need to consider some *insights into God's name.* To understand the seriousness of the Third Commandment, we should have some knowledge of how God's name was revealed to man. It is interesting to note that God revealed His name in stages. The first name, "YHWH," is from the Hebrew verb that means "to be." It is a name so holy that the people of Israel would not pronounce it. Once a year, the Priest, when he entered the Holy of Holies, would speak it. So sacred was that name, that the people tied a rope around the Priest's leg so that they might be able to drag him from the sacred spot should he be struck dead by speaking God's name. That is in vast contrast to the casual and vulgar use of God's name today. God did not reveal this name until He spoke with Moses. In Exodus 6:3 we read, "I appeared to Abraham, to Isaac and to Jacob as God Almighty, but by my name the Lord [the Hebrew word used there is "YHWH"] I did not make myself fully known to them."

The second name God used is "Adonai," which means "Lord." It is the word the Hebrews used when they were reading the Scripture and acme to "YHWH," during which they substituted "Adonai," or the exalted One. A name often used, even in the translations of the Scripture, is "Jehovah." In reality, this is a twelfth century word that combines the vowels of Adonai and the consonants of YHWH and the resulting word becomes "Jehovah." The name "Jesus," which is above all names according to the New Testament, is from the Hebrew word "Jeshua" or "Joshua" and means "Yaweh saves." To understand the sacredness of the name is to put importance on not profaning the name.

An additional insight into God's Name is that of reverencing His name. The commandment says, "You shall not misuse the name. You shall not take it up for any selfish purpose." From the hymn we sing, "His Name is Wonderful," and indeed it is. His name is to be revered because of who He is.

Iniquities with God's Name

Next, we need to consider *iniquities with God's name.* If the Third Commandment is so important, how is it applicable to us today? How is it broken? How does it fit into my life? First, there is the matter of *profanity*. To many, that is all this commandment refers to, and if a person does not use God's name in cursing, then this commandment does not apply to them. Profanity, as we know it today, was little known in the days of Moses. So sacred was the name of God that they would not have dared to profane it with a curse. The same is not true today. God's name is used with frequency by so many. It seems that Hollywood cannot make an action movie without profanity, with much of the dialogue profaning the name of God. A review of one film revealed that profanity occurred approximately every thirty-two seconds. That certainly cuts down on writing dialogue, doesn't it!

Profanity does two things. First, it reflects what the character of a person really is. The Psalmist said, "As a man thinketh in his heart, so is he" (Proverbs 23:7). Vulgar language speaks of a vulgar heart. The second thing profanity does is to give a false impression of God. For example, a common profane expression implies that God is involved in the damnation, not the salvation business. So common has this expression become that one can believe the story of the little boy who was asked, "Do you know God?" The child replied, "No, but I know His last name." When asked what God's last name was, he replied with the "D" word. How sad it is that the language of children, youth, and adults in our society has become so saturated with vulgarity and profaning the name of God.

Frivolity is another way in which we profane the name of God. By frivolously using the holy name of God or alluding to Him in a joking manner, we profane His name. Bart Simpson, in television reruns, is still demonstrating the frivolous use of God's name when he bows his head as if to say a table blessing and comes out with the following words, "We made all these things, so thanks for nothing! Amen." Often, we approach holy things not as Moses did at the burning bush, where he took off his shoes because he was standing on holy ground, but rather we approach holy things in a light and frivolous manner. A popular songwriter some years ago had us singing a song, "Have you talked to the Man Upstairs?" This seems so trivial, and in a way it was, but it has become so much, so easy that God has been reduced from a word that would not be uttered into a word that is spoken with such carelessness that the world is confused about who

He is. Are we raising a generation of children who know nothing of God except what they hear in curse words and see in movies and on television?

Perhaps *hypocrisy* is the greatest offense against the Third Commandment. G. Campbell Morgan, a biblical scholar from another era said, "The most subtle form of breaking the Third Commandment is committed by the man who says, "Lord, Lord," and does not do the things that the Lord says. Prayer without practice is blasphemy; praise without adoration violates the Third Commandment." Singing without serving is hypocrisy. Have you ever considered what God must think when He observes our behavior on Monday after we have sat in a worship service and sung, "O, How I love Jesus"?

Perhaps the most widespread example of both *frivolity* and *hypocrisy* in the use of the Lord's name is the constant exclamation typically abbreviated "OMG." First prevalent in Hollywood movies and now permeating social media and everyday conversation with the younger crowd, it is used any time something is even remotely surprising. As to its hypocrisy, it is ironic that those who use the expression "OMG" are by and large the same people who have no relationship with

Him, making their reference to Him as *their* God even more disturbing.

The Quaker theologian Elton Trueblood wrote that the most dangerous thing facing the church and the western culture is not atheism, communism, nor any other "ism." It is an acceptance of a faith without true acceptance of the founder of the faith. It is to give lip service to moral standards without taking them seriously. It is the man who broad-mindedly expresses his approval of religion but never does anything the commandments command. Such a person is like the man who never went to church but always tipped his hat as he passed one (Johnson).

Many involved in vocational church work know what it is to have someone try to manipulate us with the phrase, "God told me...," then follow with their pet agenda. God does speak and what He says needs to be shared, but not in a maneuvering way. Some television evangelists have mastered the art of "guilting" people into contributing to their ministries by evoking the name of God with their pleas for funds.

There are two final things we need to consider regarding the Third Commandment. First is the consequence of violating the commandment. The full commandment tells us that "The Lord will not hold anyone guiltless who misuses His name." It is a serious matter to be called a Christian, to take the Lord's name as your own. You need to examine yourself to see how your conduct squares with your name. The second thing we need to think about is the positive side of the commandment. We are not to misuse the name of God, but we are to use the name of God. You shall not take up the name for no good purpose, but you are to take it up.

5.

❧

REMEMBERING THE LORD'S DAY

THE FOURTH COMMANDMENT

Remember the Sabbath day by keeping it holy. Six days you shall labor and do all your work, but the seventh day is a Sabbath to the Lord your God. On it you shall not do any work, neither you, nor your son or daughter, nor your manservant or maidservant, nor your animals, nor the alien within your gates. For in six days the Lord made the heavens and the earth, the sea, and all that is in them, but he rested on the seventh day. Therefore the Lord blessed the Sabbath day and made it holy.

Exodus 20:8–11.

The story of a mythical Martian, who chooses a bright summer Sunday to fly over the Earth and do research for his thesis in comparative anthropology, is pure fantasy. The Martian wrote furiously of strangely garbed priests who gathered in large, open air arenas, before large crowds on every seventh day to perform their rituals. Still, others, no doubt the mystics, preferred to address the ball themselves with long clubs, singly or in groups of two or four, wandering in green fields. Yet, others made their way to the sea and anointed themselves with holy oil and stretched out full length in order to surrender themselves entirely to silent communion with the deity. The Martian's conclusion is that earthlings are sun worshipers.

The Martian concludes his notes with these words:

"There exists, however, a small sect of recalcitrant or heretics who do not practice sun worship. These may be identified by their habit of clothing themselves more soberly and completely than the sun worshipers. They, too, gather into groups, but only to hide from the sun in certain buildings of doubtful use, usually with windows of glass colored to keep out the light. It is not clear whether these creatures are simply unbelievers or whether they are excommunicated from sun worship for some offense—we have not been able to discover what goes on within their buildings, which may perhaps be places of punishment. But it is noteworthy that their faces and gestures show none of the almost orgiastic religious frenzy with which the sun worshipers pursue their devotions. In fact, they usually appear relaxed and even placid, thus indicating minds blank of thought or emotion..." (Davidman 48–51).

Then, Ms. Davidman asks, "Was the Martian wildly wrong or, fantastically right?"

While this is purely fiction, one would suspect that the author came closer to the truth than many of us would care to admit. On Sunday, the day that is set aside for the worship of the giver of the Ten Commandments, less than one half of those professing to be believers will be found in church. One cannot begin to estimate what percentage of those in attendance will leave a worship service without keeping God's day holy. If our nation is to experience revival, then the people of God are going to have to understand that they cannot absent themselves from the worship of God, in the house of God, without damaging their walk with God.

In its expanded form, the Fourth Commandment is the longest of the Ten Laws. It reads: "Remember the Sabbath day by keeping it holy. Six days you shall labor and do all your work, neither you, nor your son or daughter nor your manservant or maidservant, nor your animals, nor the alien within your gates. For in six days the Lord made the heavens and the earth, the sea, and all that is in them, but He rested on the seventh day. Therefore the Lord blessed the Sabbath day and made it holy" (Exodus 20:8-11).

Confirming the Day

On the subject of remembering the Lord's Day, there are *three major factors* that need to be considered. The *first factor* to be considered is *confirming the day*. A characteristic of all good leaders is that they lead by example. God is proof positive of this. He does not tell us to do that which He himself would not do. The principles of the Ten Commandments were taught before He gave them to Moses on Mount Sinai. These principles were first confirmed in the Creation story. Exodus 20:11 says, "For in six days the Lord made the heavens and the earth, the sea, and all that is in them, and rested the seventh day. Therefore the Lord blessed the Sabbath day and made it holy." The Living Bible says, "and set it aside for rest."

God worked for six days and rested on the seventh day. Thousands of years ago, as Creator and Mentor, God set in motion a model for us to live by today. These principles were confirmed in the "commute" from Egypt to the promised land, the Exodus Story. During this long journey, God led and fed His people. There were no grocery stores in the desert, yet God supplied all the needs of His people. Manna came every morning and the people were to gather it before the sun melted it away. If too much manna was gathered, it spoiled. Greedy people found themselves with messy manna—they began to get the point. As the Israelites depended upon God each day, He supplied all their needs and showed them the way. The word "manna" literally means "What is it!" Can you imagine a conversation something like this: "Hey, Mom, what is it we are having for breakfast?" Then the response, "What is it?" That is what it is!

In Exodus 16, the people of Israel are given clear instructions. They are not to go outside and gather manna on the seventh day. Only by gathering twice the amount they needed on the sixth day would they have food for the seventh day. The extra food would not spoil as the sixth day turned into the Sabbath. Why? It was to be a Sabbath unto the Lord.

The Covenant

A *second factor* to be considered is found in the *covenant* God made with His people in Exodus 31:13, when He says, "Say to the Israelites, 'You must observe my Sabbaths. This will be a sign between me and you for the generations to come, so you may know that I am the Lord, who makes you holy.'" *Observing* the commanded day of rest was essential if the people of God were going to experience the blessing of being a covenant people.

The Commandment itself is a *third confirmation* of the day of rest and worship. As someone once well said, these are not the "Ten Suggestions," they are the Ten Commandments. God straightforwardly confirms that we are to both labor and worship and rest. It is an essential ingredient to our health, both physically and spiritually. By example and teaching, God directs us to keep His special day holy.

Throughout the centuries, as well as today, there

have been those who insisted upon cheapening the day. A study of the history of the nation to whom the Commandments were given reveals ways in which the Sabbath day was abused and cheapened. It began with the Israelites taking the day lightly. The book of Nehemiah contains the story of many who had been captured and carried off into captivity, later returning to their homeland. When Nehemiah returned to his homeland, he found the people treating the Sabbath day like just another day; they had no interest in worship or keeping the Sabbath.

The same is very true today. A television advertisement for a pain reliever depicts a hatmaker going about his trade with his wife extolling how the product has enabled him to work six days a week. He is then seen with his fishing gear and heard saying, "After all, a man has to fish sometimes." This so aptly describes so many people's attitude toward God's holy day. It has become a day to do as I please. I may have a responsibility at my church but once something comes up which appeals to me more than attending church, then I will just do it. After all, I deserve a break. We have lost a sense of loyalty to God, His day, and our sense of duty in faithfully discharging our service to

Him. Missing church without even having a pang of conscience has become easy for so many.

As long as the people of God view the special day of God as something they determine the use of rather than following His direction, we cannot expect the winds of revival to come sweeping across our land. When the people of God begin to return to the House of God with humble hearts and broken wills, then and only then, the Spirit of God will move among us with might and power.

At the time of Jesus, the religious leaders had made the keeping of the Sabbath an unbearable system of legalism. There were one-thousand five-hundred twenty-one things one was expressly forbidden to do on the Sabbath, including rescuing a drowning man. One might pick up a child, but if the child had an object in his hand, one would have violated the law by bearing a burden. Women were forbidden to look in a mirror lest they discover a gray hair and pluck it out. Jesus seemed to be constantly in trouble with the religious leaders of His time for breaking the Sabbath. By His actions and His announcements, Jesus placed a different emphasis on the Lord's Day. He worshiped, He healed, and when called into question, He set forth this pronouncement, "The Sabbath was made for man, not man for the Sabbath" (Mark 2:27).

Puritanical tradition dictated that Sunday was a day when nothing fun could take place. It was boring. One preacher said the most exciting thing he could do on Sunday was sit on the front porch and listen to his hair grow! I can remember wanting to play baseball on Sundays. I was not forbidden to play, in fact we had some hot games out in the pasture, but my upbringing made it very hard to play on an organized team, such as the American Legion team I played on between my junior and senior years in high school. I don't think I ever made a hit on a Sunday. I finally left the team at mid-season; they went to the finals of the national tournament.

Many modern-day atheists will trace their lack of belief to the endless, dull, bleak Sundays in a nega- tively "Christian" household, which made a child's life seem hardly worth living.

We have seen a great shift in the observance of Sun- day in our lifetimes. Jerry Vines states, "Our grandfa- thers called it the Sabbath; our father called it Sunday and we call it the weekend and it is getting weaker all the time" (Vines 45). We have gone from blue laws to blue-light specials. How sad it is that a faith that is supposed to bring one joy has driven so many away by its rigidity. What a tragedy that so many professing believers treat the Lord's day so lightly. There is, however, a happy medium in between taking the commandment too lightly or too legalistically.

We can remember the Sabbath by celebrating the day. The first recipients of the Ten Commandments understood their meanings. For more than four hundred years, they had been slaves with no time off from work. No day was set aside for rest and fellowship with God. From Mount Sinai came the word from God that they were to observe a Sabbath, a word that literally means rest.

The Work

There are two essential elements in the Fourth Commandment. First, there is the matter of *work*. Contrary to popular belief, work is not a punishment that came because of the fall of man. It was always God's intention that man and woman work. They were placed in the Garden and told to care for it. Work is an essential part of our well being. We have made it far too easy for people to "get by" without working. We are admonished in the New Testament that if one will not work, he is not to eat. That means, the able-bodied person who can work but will not is not to be taken care of by society. Does this sound unkind? No, it is just the opposite. Work brings dignity into one's life. The Fourth Commandment admonishes us that we are to work.

On the other hand, the Fourth Commandment tells us there is a time to stop working, a time to rest, to cease from one's labor. One writer says, "God told us 3,000 years ago what production analysts have concluded only recently; that reasonably spaced and carefully used work breaks, clearly increase productivity" (Hybels 45).

The Worshiping

The second element in the Fourth Commandment is the matter of *worshiping*. Though nothing is said in the commandment about worship, it is clearly implied, and we know from reading the scripture that the Hebrew people understood this. Worship was very much a part of the Sabbath observance. How do we as God's people today celebrate the Sabbath? There are three suggested ways. There is the matter of the First Day. Why do we worship on Sunday, instead of Saturday or the Sabbath. The Old Testament Sabbath was from sundown Friday until sundown on Saturday. It was on the first day of the week, Sunday, when our Lord arose from the grave. It was on Sunday that many of his post-resurrection appearances took place. There is no command for the day to be changed, but we hear Paul in 1 Corinthians 16:2 saying, "On the first day of every week, each one of you should set aside a sum of money in keeping with his income."

This second element in celebrating the Lord's Day is the matter of the *first fruits*. Paul speaks to this in his letters to the Corinthians. We are to gather on the first day and are to bring with us the first fruits of our labor, our tithes and offerings, which belong to God. That is to be part of our celebration. We should allow our children to participate in giving and teach them to give from their allowances or the monies they earn.

Our tithes and offerings are a demonstration of our first love, showing that we are willing to place God above everything else in our lives. Such love was in evidence among the first-century Christians. In contrast to this expression of preeminent devotion to God, the Romans thought they should be holding orgies as part of their worship, essentially gratifying their own lusts. They were so caught up in their form of worship that they could not understand their Christian friends' objections. Prayer, praise, fellowship, and joy all should be elements of our worship. We need to prepare ourselves for worship; participate in worship and preserve our time of worship. We need to be prepared physically and spiritually before we come to worship. We need to participate in the worship and preserve what we have learned from that experience by thinking about it during the week and sharing what we have learned with others.

When we gather for worship, three things should take place. We should be *chastened*, *challenged*, and *changed* (Hybels 47). Sometimes, someone will say, "You really stepped on my toes this morning." No, I didn't. That is not my job; it is the job of the Holy Spirit. He will be *chastening* some about your lack of a daily walk with Him. For others, it is concerning your casual or indifferent attitude toward worship and church attendance. Others know they need to be using their talents for God. Still, others lack in financial giving. If He is chastening, you are hearing the message.

He speaks very plainly.

Not only should we be chastened, but we should also be *challenged*. Challenged to stretch in our walk with Him. Each of us needs to be challenged in our work. God is never satisfied with the status quo; He wants us to be constantly growing. He is also challenging some of us to listen to His chastening and be obedient.

Finally, we need to be *changed*. Some need open-heart surgery. We need the fresh blood of Jesus Christ coursing through our spiritual veins and we need to be changed. Our walk needs to be changed; our gods need to be changed from the gods of the world to the God of the universe. Some of us need our motivation changed; serving from obligation is not a good reason, serving from guilt is not either. God wants us to remember His day and be chastened, challenged, and changed.

6.

⌒

RESPECTING THE FAMILY

THE FIFTH COMMANDMENT

Honor your father and your mother, so that you may
live long in the land the lord your God is giving you.

Exodus 20:12.

It was obvious when he walked into my office, closed the door, sat down across the desk from me and looked into my face with eyes that were already tearing that this was not a social call. My first thought was, "Have I done something to offend him?"

"Pastor," he said, "that Father's Day sermon of yours yesterday really got to me. I have got to have some help." For the next hour I listened to a very successful businessman pour out his heart about his failure as a father.

"Pastor, when you talked about your pastor father, his influence on your life, I saw myself as just the opposite. You talked about playing on a summer softball team with your father. I never even played catch with one of my sons. I never once did anything like that with my sons. What really got to me was when you talked about spending Saturday mornings in your father's study preparing the sermons you would both preach the next day. Pastor, I never once sat down with either of my sons and seriously talked with them about anything. When you talked about your father's encouraging words, all I could think about was my yelling at the boys," he expressed.

He continued to pour out his heart, and I said very little, just listened as he hurt. He reached a place where he broke down and sobbed. I walked around the desk, put my arms around him, and cried with him. It took some time for him to compose himself enough to continue. "Pastor," he said, "I have two boys. I don't even know where one of them is. The other one is a drug addict. They both have been married and divorced. I have grandchildren I haven't seen in years. Pastor, I remember the sermon you preached on honoring you father and mother. My boys don't honor me because I was not an honorable father. Is there any hope for my situation?"

He was transferred shortly after and I have no knowledge of what became of his determination to try to, in his words, "right his wrongs."

Ten Commandments as a Light

What I do know is that the Ten Commandments are important for every new generation. That which was morally right or wrong in the Old Testament is pertinent and practical for today. God's character never fluctuates from one generation to the next. God's House rules are always the same. We need to remind ourselves that we should be cautious and courteous in the way in which we pass these commandments to each new generation. The *Ten Commandments serve as a light.* They illuminate our path, giving us the ability to see down the dark trails of life and avoid the things that would make us stumble. In Ephesians 5:15–17 we are told, "Be very careful, then, how you live—not as unwise but as wise, making the most of every opportunity, because the days are evil. Therefore, do not be foolish, but understand what the Lord's will is."

Ten Commandments as a Leash

Not only are God's commandments a light, but they are also a *leash*, reminding us of our limits. The commandments restrain us and keep us from moral compromise and falling into sin. We need to know where the boundaries are. The Ten Commandments keep us from hurting ourselves and allow us to live in freedom. It may seem that boundaries and freedom do not mix, but the fact is that for freedom to exist, there must be boundaries.

Ten Commandments as a Level

In addition, the commandments serve as a *level* to give us a clear standard by which to evaluate our behavior. The commandments tell us wrong from right without debate. Just as a carpenter's level shows him when a board is straight, the commandments clearly tell us when our life is contrary to God's Character (Peel 31). Galatians 3:24 says, "So the law was put in charge to lead us to Christ that we might be justified by faith."

Today in America, the time is ripe for the light, leash, and leveling effect of the Fifth Commandment. A noted scholar said, "Today's children are tyrants.

They disobey their parents, gobble their food and tyrannize their teachers." Socrates spoke those words in 400 B.C.. It seemed that the Greeks were in need of a sweeping revival, just as we are in need of revival today. If revival is to come to America, should it not first begin with revival in our homes? Remember the parable of the prodigal son. When the repentant son returned home, revival and joy raised the roof of the father's home. The once "holy terror" had come home with a fresh understanding of a holy God and honor for his father and mother.

Upon close examination, the place and prominence of the Fifth Commandment is not accidental. It occupies a special position. It stands at the head of the list of commandments dealing with our daily and ongoing relationship with the people in our personal worlds. This commandment serves as a bridge between the first table of commandments that teach us about our relationship to God and the second table of commandments because it is from our parents that we learn about trust, protection, provision, love, and positive or negative attitudes about God.

It is proper order that our relationship to God be put first in the table of the commandments. We must have no other gods before Him. The proper order in the second table is for the family to be in first place. The commandments must be in this order. Parents witness the precious experience of our lives coming into existence through the miracle of birth. Then, they seek to bless our lives as they nurture and care for us. Sometimes we think our parents are overprotective and too strict. Parents must set the ground rules and restrictions by which their children live.

The Fifth Commandment places much emphasis on the responsibility of parents to be honorable. Parents who have the attitude and actions of "do as I say, not as I do" will never instill a code of honor in the hearts of their children. Godly parents will always seek to honor God and set a godly example before their children. It does not mean that all children who are raised by godly parents will always live for the Lord. Adam and Eve, God's very first children were prodigals. But parents who rear their children in the "nurture and admonition of the Lord," will see a greater percentage of their children come back to God and their moral upbringing after a "bottom out" experience.

A free translation of Ephesians 6:4 says, "Parents don't drive your children nuts!" (Briscoe 82). Parents must take their parenting seriously so their children will know they are the parents that God ordained them to be. Children find it easy to honor parents who are honorable.

> Parents need to balance criticism with praise. There ought to be more strokes than pokes, more bragging than nagging. Your children learn what you teach them at home. If you teach them criticism, they learn to condemn. If you teach them hostility, they learn to fight. If you teach them shame, they learn to feel guilt. If you teach them tolerance, they learn patience. If you teach them praise, they learn to be appreciative. If you teach them security, they learn to trust. Parents are to respond. That simply puts the responsibility on the parents (Vines 62–63).

The Fifth Commandment is a bridge between the two tables of law and basic to the keeping of the laws which follow. All of the commandments have implied promises. Obedience to the law keeps one in a right relationship with the Father. It does not bring one into the relationship, but it keeps the lines of communication open. The Fifth Commandment contains a straight-forward, stated reward for obedience: the promise of perpetuity in the land. The Promised Land was given to the Israelites for forever, but only on one condition: obedience. This commandment tells them, "Honor your father and your mother, so that you may live long in the land the Lord your God is giving you." Note, it says "is giving you." It is a process, and their obedience is part of the process. Prosperity came with obedience. Deportation came with disobedience.

The Promise of Prosperity

In the Deuteronomy account of the Ten Commandments, the obedient child is *promised prosperity* in their life. The Living Bible states, "if you do, you shall have a long, prosperous life in the land" (Deuteronomy 5:15). The generation that cuts itself off from the godliness of the previous generation will have to deal with the results of godlessness. You cannot carry bitterness toward your parent and have a healthy home yourself. No matter how justified you may be in having bitter feelings, they are baggage you cannot afford to carry. God says that when we obey our parents, we will have a more prosperous life. Dwight L. Moody, the great

90

evangelist, said, "I have lived sixty years and I have learned one thing if I have not learned anything else; no man ever prospers who does not honor his father and mother."

Obedience to the command assures one of pleasantries in daily living. It is God's intention that the family relationship be a happy one. How wonderful it is when parents and children live together and relate together in a Godly spirit of love and cooperation. The book of Proverbs is filled with passages that deal with both the joy and the hurt that come into the family unit.

We need to examine our family relationship. Do you look forward to spending time together? Is it a pleasant atmosphere or a battleground, a heaven on earth or a bit of hell? Do not forget that a family is a two-way street. Children are told to obey their parents and parents are told not to exasperate their children. Living in a home where all are in right relationship with the first four commandments will assure that the Fifth Commandment is being kept, and this pleasures the Lord. Colossians 3:20 says, "Children obey your parents in everything, for this pleases the Lord." Just like any parent is pleased when their children obey, so the heavenly Father is pleased when He observes His children being obedient.

How do we honor our father and our mother? The starting place is in respecting their authority. The first chapter of Romans, especially verses 28–32, tells of every terrible sin one can imagine, and in the midst of that list are the words "they disobey their parents." Verse 32 states, "those who do such things deserve death." It is a serious offense against God to not respect one's parents.

For some, respecting your parents is especially difficult because of parents or a parent, who for one reason or another, have not earned the right to be respected. While serving as Chaplain in a Texas State Children's Home, I announced I was going to preach a series of sermons on the Ten Commandments. I started preparing the series and the thought hit me, "I am going to have to preach on the Fifth Commandment to a group of more than three hundred children, most of whom had been removed from their parents care." I found myself on the horns of a dilemma! Through prayer and study, God began to show me that the child is not accountable for the conduct of the parent, but for their own conduct. The office of parenthood is honorable regardless of the conduct of the parent. Parents are to be honored for the role they fill. You are to respect them for what you can respect, and you exemplify your walk with the God of the commandments by your behavior. You respect the position of father or mother, whether the person in that position is honorable or not.

For this reason, it is so important for parents to honor the role that God has given them. Children receive their first perceptions about God from their parents. Calling God their heavenly Father is very difficult for many because they had such a poor father role model. Parenting is an awesome responsibility. Parents must take seriously their respect for the authority of God and teach respect for authority to their children.

A little boy was told by his father to sit down in the car and put on his seat belt. The child said, "I am not going to do it!" The mother grabbed the boy by the earlobe and lowered him into the seat saying, "Basically what your dad means, Johnny, is that either sit down and buckle up, or you're in big trouble." Wisely, Johnny sits down and buckles his seat belt. As he does so, he glares at his father and mumbles, "I might be sitting down on the outside, but I'm standing up on the inside!" (Hybels 56).

When I was in high school, a boy said to me," I

hear your 'old man' is a preacher, is that right?" I replied, "No, I don't have an 'old man.' I have a father, and he is the pastor of the First Baptist Church." Give respect to whom respect is due, and respect is due to the parent. In honoring our father and mother, we need to reverence them for their care. When we sit down and contemplate all they have done for us, we find that most of us have piled up a tremendous debt to them. The cost of raising a child is tremendous. The hours of tending to us during sickness; the many favors done; the sacrifices made, put us in a position for which we have much to say, "Thank you."

Repay by Conduct

A third way in which we honor our parents is to repay them by our *conduct*. The way we behave reflects on our upbringing. Public school teachers will tell you that they can tell a great deal about the home a child comes from by observing the child's behavior at school. Philippians 2:14 says, "Do everything without complaining and arguing." Christian children need to learn that if you are going to be Christian around the church, you must start by being a Christian at home

(Vines 65).

I grew up in "Small Town," USA, the son of a Baptist preacher. Everyone in town knew who I was and whose son I was. There were a few things I might have done in my teenage years if I had not been so aware of the fact that my conduct reflected upon my father. The commandment does not say to honor your parents until you are eighteen years old. It says that we are to continue to repay our parents by giving them the respect their position deserves.

Finally, we need to radiate love in this parent-child relationship. The word "radiate" perhaps best describes how God wants this relationship to be. This word conjures up images of warmth radiating from the fireplace, light radiating from a lamp. The word sounds warm and fuzzy and depicts what our homes ought to be. I have received many cards and messages, two of which come instantly to mind. One was a banner I found hanging on my office door from a group of four-year-old children who wrote, "We love you, Pastor." The other was a card from my son-in-law, which read in part, "Dear Mom and Pop...you have accepted me as one of your very own right from the beginning. You have welcomed me, cherished me, and done so much for me. For these things I give you sincere and heartfelt thanks. I have accepted you as one of my own. I love you dearly." Signed, "Your Son."

I have stood by the graveside of many parents and heard their children say, " I hope he knew I loved him" and "I hope she knew I loved her." Do not wait until it is too late to tell them they are loved. A man took his wife and son to a lake for a vacation. While the mother was fixing a meal in the house, the father and son went out on the lake in a boat. A sudden storm came up; clouds covered the sun, and there was darkness over the lake as the waves began to billow. The son and father saw a light the mother had put in the window and the father said, "Son, I am going to row. You keep your eyes on the light. Help me go in the direction of the light." They followed the light and made it to the house safely. When they arrived home, the mother was there to greet them. The son said, "Mom, we came home safely because we steered by your light" (Vines 68).

Parents are to keep the light lit to guide their children safely in life. The light will guide them in making the right choices. It will guide them in a proper walk with God. It also will guide them in becoming the right type of parents for their own children. Children are to keep their eyes on the light their parents have placed in the window. They are to keep walking in the right direction. God prospers those who keep His commandments.

7.

❧

REVERENCING LIFE

THE SIXTH COMMANDMENT

You shall not murder.

Exodus 20:13

A young man was driving an emerald green Mercedes at 1:30 a.m. on the California San Diego Freeway near Bel-Air, when he pulled his car onto a desolate off-ramp. This was a decision that would ultimately cost him his life. The twenty-seven-year-old young man was killed by a single gunshot to the head. The nation was shocked as newscasters declared that Ennis Cosby, the only son of Bill Cosby, was the victim of this brutal, cold-blooded murder. Sorrow welled up in our hearts for the family, as we saw them confronted with a "lightning storm" of camera flashes as the media hunted for a front-page story. Mental pictures of the television character, Theo Huxtable, flashed through our thoughts.

This was not a Cosby TV show; this was real life and a happy ending was not being set up for the audience. This random act of senseless violence had taken a very precious thing from a father and mother, a family, and, in essence, from all of us. Murder is an awful thing! The Sixth Commandment deals with the subject of life, its sanctity, and our responsibility for treating life with reverence. We are most familiar with the words in the King James Version, which reads, "Thou shalt not kill." Some modern translations read, "You shall not murder," which is a better translation.

The Sixth Commandment forms the foundation of all civilization and human government. The day that modern man completely loses his understanding of the value of human life is the day we begin living like the "Planet of the Apes." Forgive me, I take that back, because even apes have a higher appreciation for life than a person who commits a "drive-by" shooting into a crowd of innocent bystanders or throws a newborn baby into a trash dumpster.

Facts of Life

Let us examine the *facts of life*. One of the first lessons that the Bible teaches us about life is that God is life, the first fact of life. Jeremiah 10:10 says, "But the Lord is the True God; he is the living God." Over and over, the Bible declares that our God is the living God. Life itself belongs to God Almighty. It was He who spoke life into existence. "In the beginning God created," and His crowning creation was life.

Out of nothing came everything, because God willed it into existence. Things seen and unseen by the human eye came into existence because God, the Creator, spoke. He said, "Let there be light," and that light is still traveling today. Science tells us that we live in an ever-expanding universe. God did not have to create life. It came as an act of the personal and free will of our Creator because God is not only life, but also God is love. Genesis 1:27 says, "So God created man in his own image, in the image of God he created them, male and female, he created them." Every man's life is God's life. Our lives belong to God, and that answers the question, "What is the big deal about life?" Genesis 9:6 says it clearly, "Whoever sheds the blood of man, by man shall his blood be shed; for in the image of God has God made man."

We are not highly evolved animals without a soul. Each person has the unique ability to know God; communicate with God; follow God's plan for their lives; and live for God's glory. To destroy what God loves is an insult to God Almighty. Sinful man has an image problem when it comes to life. First John 4:8 says, "God is love." This is the second fact of life. Love craved expression, therefore, He created man for fellowship. The third fact of life is that God is lawgiving. The Psalmist said, "The law of the Lord is perfect, reviving the soul. The statutes of the Lord are trustworthy, making wise the simple. The percepts of the Lord are right, giving joy to the heart" (Psalm 19:7–8). God-loving, law-abiding citizens do not have to live in a state of chaos and anarchy. Our God loves life and has set boundaries for our own good. The nations that have ignored these laws now lie in rubble and have gone down in history as nations of fools.

Fatalities of Life

Next, we need to look at the *fatalities of life*. Sometimes, death occurs and is not intentional and flowing out of a heart of hate. Are grace and mercy allowed in

102

some cases? For example, take the case of accidental killing. In the Old Testament, in Deuteronomy 19, a program of cities of refuge was established, which were places for a person to live, who accidentally had taken a life. A person who accidentally killed another could flee to the city of refuge and remain there until his case was carefully dealt with, providing a time for emotions to cool down.

Authorized Killing

In addition, God spoke concerning *authorized killing*. Previously, we addressed the fact that the proper translation of the verse renders the word as murder and not kill. There is not a prohibition against all killing. For example, the Sixth Commandment does not, as many believe, prohibit capital punishment. In fact, the Bible sets forth teachings that support the taking of life. Genesis 9:6 reads, "Whoever shed man's blood, by man his blood shall be shed." There is not a prohibition against war. Deuteronomy 20 contains God's instructions for war. As reprehensible as war is, sometimes it cannot be avoided. The Sixth Commandment is not an argument for pacifism.

Today, we find many who use the Sixth Commandment as an argument against the killing of animals. A large social movement has evolved surrounding the issue of the taking of animals' lives in medical experiments, by hunters and even for food. Whatever one's convictions may be on this subject, the use of the Sixth Commandment is not justification for one's position.

At-Risk Killing

A fourth area which needs to be addressed is "*at-risk killing*" or killing in self-defense. There are those who carry this commandment to extreme, who would not allow even for defending themselves and their family. I read of a person, who was awakened in the middle of the night by a noise downstairs. He took his hunting rifle and slipped down the stairs and came upon a burglar. He shouted at the man, " Friend, I would not harm you for anything in the world, but you are standing where I am about to shoot" (Huffman 87). Exodus 22:2 says, "If the thief is found breaking in, and he is struck so that he dies, the defender is not guilty of bloodshed." Life is sacred. It is not to be taken lightly, but God is a God of grace. We must not make His laws what they are not.

"You shall not murder" speaks of life being taken in numerous ways. We live in a society with an attitude of murder all around us. "For from within, out of men's hearts, come evil thoughts, sexual immorality, theft, murder..." (Mark 7:21). Much is being said concerning the "angry young people"; gangs value life as cheap, having the attitude that a life for a life is quite prevalent. Jesus spoke in the Sermon on the Mount, Matthew (5:21–22), on the attitude of murder. He said, "You have heard that it was said to those of old, 'You shall not murder, and whoever murders will be in danger of judgment.' But I say to you that whoever is angry with his brother without a cause shall be in danger of the judgment.'"

The attitude of murder leads to anger-murder that springs forth from a heart filled with hate and murder. The example of Cain and Abel, the first murder, gives us the tragic results of unresolved anger, referring to the attitude of murder of which Jesus spoke. Our current laws categorize murder and make a distinction between premeditated murder and murder committed in a fit of rage. The person who is killed is just as dead and the killer has violated the sacredness of life created in God's image, regardless of how our law characterizes the murder.

One of the most divisive issues in our nation today deals with abortive murder. There are many honestly held opinions about when life begins. These opinions make the "Right to Life" issues so difficult for many. The Scripture presents life within the womb. Speaking to the prophet Jeremiah, God said, "Before I formed you in the womb, I knew you; before you were born, I set you apart; I appointed you as a prophet to the nations" (Jeremiah 1:5). One can place one's hands on the abdomen of a pregnant woman and feel the life created by God moving within her. "Roe v. Wade" opened the door for a few abortions in extreme cases, and now, millions of abortions later, we discover that once again the door has opened; the sinfulness of man has pushed the floodgate open further.

The same rationale that led to the termination of unwanted pregnancies is being used on the elderly and the terminally ill. This could be referred to as aged murder. Once it is legal and accepted, the abuses of life will abound. Some of the most difficult decisions families ever make center around "when do we pull the plug." I have been there with my family and felt the division that comes with such a decision. This is not an easy decision, and it will become increasingly difficult as new methods for prolonging life become available. Medical science is giving us lengthier and greater quality of life, but it also is presenting us with more difficult choices. Always, the sacredness of life must be preserved; however, it must be tempered with the reality that life does come to an end. There is "a time to die." A good relationship between the family and the doctors and discussions among the family before the situation arises could help make these decisions less difficult, though never easy. A living-will helps make this difficult decision easier.

The world has been exposed to atrocious murders. The mass killings of Hitler and his desire for a master race resulted in some of the greatest atrocities ever known. We have been appalled by the policy of "Ethnic Cleansing." The destruction of the World Trade Center using airplanes as weapons, the sabotage of other airplanes, and senseless mass murders of school children and teachers by other students serve to keep us ever mindful that the Sixth Commandment is not outdated.

Years ago, Dr. Jack Kevorkian made headlines evading state laws by performing abortions and assisting others in taking their lives. That has become almost commonplace today. Thousands take their own lives without assistance. Numerous other suicides go undetected. Suicide is the ultimate insult to God and your family. It is an abandonment of the post that God has assigned to you, a statement that He no longer can be trusted. It often saddles the family with a lifetime of questioning where they had failed and what could have been done to prevent the death.

There is also what could be termed as apathetic murder. Jesus spoke of this type of murder in Matthew 25:42–43 saying, "I was hungry and you gave me nothing to eat; I was thirsty and you gave me nothing to drink; I was a stranger and you did not take me in; naked and you did not clothe me; sick, and in prison, and you did not visit me." A hurting, hungry world has a right to look to the people of God, who put a premium on life, and ask, "Do you not care that we are dying?"

In the Old Testament, we hear God saying to his people, "Behold, I have set before you a choice... choose life or choose death." Genesis 2:7 says that God breathed into man the breath of life. He made man for eternity. There is the matter of spiritual death, which is a physical reality. We are told that "it is appointed unto man, once to die and after death, the judgment" (Hebrews 9:27). It is sometimes said, "Man will live eternally, either in heaven or in hell." This is not true; the person who has not accepted Jesus Christ as Savior, will not live eternally, he will die eternally. The Bible warns us of a second death, the Lake of Fire, eternal separation from God. One's failure to respond to God's life in Christ is the ultimate committing of "Spiritual Suicide" (Huffman 86).

On the other hand, Jesus speaks of eternal life on numerous occasions. He tells us in John 10:10 that He has "come that we might have life and have it to the full." Life is intended by God to be rich and rewarding; life is to be lived eternally in fellowship with Him. As there is eternal death, there is eternal life. Jesus Christ is the way the truth and the life. Life and life eternal are in His hands. He holds the keys to life. He has laid down His life for our sakes. Through the shedding of His blood, we have life. In an interview with Mother Teresa, Robert Schuller recounted her vivid story of an earthquake victim in Armenia. She said, "There was a mother who was caught under the debris, trapped for eight days with a little child, maybe two or three years old. When they found the mother, they saw that she had cut her finger and she had fed the child with her own blood, putting her finger in the child's mouth. Yes, she fed the child for eight days with her own blood" (Schuller).

Life is from God; it is sacred, and it must always be treated as a precious gift with which we have been entrusted. We need to examine the positive side of this commandment. Not only are we to not murder, but also, we are to live life to its fullest. Questions remain! Who are you living for? What are you living for? What kind of example are you setting for those who look at the way you live? If you think that the Sixth Commandment does not apply to you in any way, have you considered that you are guilty of the death of Jesus? It was for your sins that He died. Are you going to allow His death to be in vain or are you going to accept His offer of forgiveness and commit yourself to Him and live in fellowship with Him?

8.

~

ROMANCING THE HOME

THE SEVENTH COMMANDMENT

You shall not commit adultery.

Exodus 20:14

❚❚ Dearly Beloved, we are gathered together in the sight of God and this company, to join together this man and this woman in the bonds of holy matrimony..." Many of times, I have repeated those words as I stood facing a beaming bride and nervous groom. Every one of those couples stood before me with the highest expectations. She had found her "Prince Charming"; he had found his "Cinderella." Following the ceremony, they would climb into their "pumpkin coach" and ride off together and live happily ever after.

It happens that way in fairy tales, but in real life the

111

situation is often very different. Sometime after the "I do's" and the wedding kiss comes the reality of the real world. There is more to marriage than two people being madly in love with each other. Somewhere following the I do's, the wedding gifts, and the honeymoon comes the reality of real life—the day to day living together as husband and wife. As in anything worthwhile, for a marriage to be good, hard work is involved. "For better or for worse" are more than just filler words in the marriage ceremony. These words describe an important part of the relationship that requires work. It is not, as one young bride said at the wedding rehearsal, "I'll take him for better, but if he gets worse, I'll kill him." The gloomy statistics show that many are living out the drama of broken relationships. What started out as a little bit of heaven has turned into hell on earth.

If America is to experience revival, there must be a rediscovery of God, a reverence for the family, and a re-establishment of the important position of the home. We live in a society that places a premium on romance. More and more the home is less and less the center of romance. In fact, there are those who would question if there is anything glamorous or romantic about the home. There should be. In fact, the romance that led to marriage should continue to blossom and become sweeter as the years go by.

The Seventh Commandment minces no words. It has no disclaimers or exceptions. It simply says, "You shall not commit adultery." It puts a premium on protecting the sanctity of the marriage relationship. In the Old Testament setting, adultery was a prohibiting of sexual relations by a man with a married woman, who was not his wife. It did not deal with his conduct with an unmarried woman. The reason being that a woman was considered property; there was indeed a double standard! Jesus raised the woman to personhood and equality. In the New Testament, the definition of adultery changed to include sexual relations in which at least one participant is married to someone else. Lest some of you think this definition lets you off the hook, it does not. The New Testament raised the standards for all. Not only for the married, but also for single adults. The Greeks gave us the word, "porne," the root word of pornography, which means "fornication" and describes sexual activity between unmarried individuals. We need to understand, as Christians, that sexual activity in any form outside of marriage violates the

Law of God. There are no extenuating circumstances that nullify God's words. God simply says, "don't do it."

Marital Addition

There is *mathematics to marriage.* That may sound strange, but when God established the home, He built it upon some divine mathematical principles. We need to understand God's principle of *marital addition.* In Genesis 2:24 (KJV), God said, "and they shall be one flesh." The two become one. Only in God's addition can one plus one equal one. Failure to understand this principle creates many problems. Two becoming one in marriage addresses both the spiritual and physical union. For the home to be what it should be, both the spiritual and the physical are important. As two individuals grow spiritually together, they grow closer together. Only in God can two wills become one when added together. Only in God can two spirits become one when added together. Some know what it is to grow in a relationship until you know what the other person is thinking before they say it. That is a part of God's equation of two becoming one.

Contrary to what many of this generation believe, they did not discover sex. God created it and when he declared that His creation of man and woman was good, that included all His instructions to them. One of those instructions was that they were to "become one flesh." Inherent in that instruction is the act of being joined together sexually. It was a part of God's good creation. Ecclesiastes 9:9 says, "Enjoy life with your wife, whom you love..." So explicitly does the Song of Solomon depict the joy of love between husband and wife, that the Jewish Rabbis decreed it was not to be read by men under the age of thirty. Even a casual reading of God's Word destroys the false teaching that sex is dirty. It is only dirty when it is outside of God's mathematical formula. Love is to be fulfilling.

Marital Subtraction

We also need to understand God's principle of *marital subtraction*. Genesis 2:24 says, "That is why a man leaves his father and mother and is united to his wife..." At the same time, one is being added to one and becoming one, two are being subtracted from two and becoming one. The husband is being subtracted from the home of his parents and the wife from the home of her parents so that they may establish one home together under God's direction. Your spouse is to be your number one personal relationship above all family relationships.

Marital Multiplication

The third part of God's mathematical formula is the principle of *marital multiplication*. "They shall be fruitful and multiply," was part of God's instruction for marriage. Procreation is central in God's plan for the continuation of humankind. This is a very special privilege. Love is to be fruitful.

Marital Division

Marital division is the final part of the divine equation, the first three mathematical principles are declared to be good. There is no place for division in God's plan; one plus one equals one, but one plus one plus one equals one too many and leads to division. Hebrews 13:4 tells us, "Marriage should be honored by all, and the marriage bed kept pure, for God will judge the adulterer and all the sexually immoral." Division comes when a marriage partner allows someone from the outside to come in and break the bonds of holy matrimony. Love is to be faithful.

The sin of the adulterer strikes at the heart of God's very first institution. It is the menace of marriage! Not a single one of the Ten Commandments is inserted as a filler. Each of them is essential in God's planning for the success of life. When God says, "You shall not commit adultery," He does so because He understands the damage it brings to a home. When adultery takes place, trust is broken. At the marriage altar, sacred vows are spoken and commitments are made. Adultery is the ultimate breaching of these commitments. It has been said that trust is the immune system to any relationship. When trust is lost, the relationship is on the verge of collapse.

When adultery takes place, truth is breached. It is amazing how we rationalize, how we can justify that which we know is wrong. In our society, we have come to accept certain things as just a part of the way things are. Standards are lowered, and we accept that which is unacceptable. In recently re-watching the movie "The Bridges of Madison County," I found myself wanting the Clint Eastwood and Meryl Streep characters to become romantically involved. It looked so right. Very quickly, however, the preacher side of me took over as I remembered the couples I have counseled after they had succumbed to that temptation and the devastation it played in their lives. It was obviously a Hollywood fantasy, as phony as any. When adultery takes place, the enemy has won. We have lost. Temptation is a part of life; the devil sees to that. Temptation is not the sin; it is what follows the tempting that is sin.

Adultery is a *sin* against your heart. In Matthew 5:27–28, Jesus says, "You have heard that it was said, 'Do not commit adultery.' But I tell you that anyone who looks at a woman lustfully has already committed adultery with her in his heart." Second Peter 2:14 says, "With eyes full of adultery, they never stop sinning." It starts in the heart, the American Standard Version reads, "Then the lust, when it hath conceived, beareth sin" (James 1:15). It is conceived in the heart. You cannot fill your minds with "Playboy" magazine, romance novels, R-rated movies, and soap operas without your mind thinking that which it should not be thinking. Adultery is a sin against your heart.

Adultery is a sin against your home. The commandments are repeated to the Children of Israel, as they are preparing to enter the Promised Land. God tells them in Deuteronomy 6, "These are the commands,...the Lord your God directed me to teach...so that you, your children and their children after them may fear the Lord your God as long as you live by keeping all his decrees and commands that I give you, and so that you may enjoy long life. "Adultery strikes at the very foundation of the family. That which hurts the family destroys society.

Adultery is a sin against your *heritage*. Deuteronomy 6 spoke of your children and their children. A broken marital relationship breaks the family relationship. Statistics reveal that children of divorce are more likely to experience divorce when they marry. Why? Because they model what has been modeled for them. There is a song that asks the haunting question, "Who is going to teach our children's children?" The answer is we do in part. We teach them by the heritage we leave. The book of Proverbs tells us "Like father, like son." Implied is "Like mother, like daughter." How many times do we hear, "He is just like his daddy, or she is just like her mother"? I often tell those preparing for marriage that they can get a good idea of the kind of husband or wife they are getting by looking at the parents of their intended life partner.

Adultery is a sin against your *honor*. Each time I perform a wedding, I ask questions that call for an "I do" or an "I will." I ask the bride and groom to repeat vows after me. They are, before God and those assembled, making sacred vows, putting their honor on the line. In recent years, much has been said about whether marital infidelity should be an issue in political elections. Listen to the words of Proverbs 6:32 and we have the answer. "A man who commits adultery has no sense; whoever does so destroys himself." Faced with the advances of his master's wife, young Joseph says, "No one is greater in this house than I am. My master has withheld nothing from me except you, because you are his wife. How then could I do such a wicked thing and sin against God?" (Genesis 39:9). His honor was at stake, and he knew that honor is compromised when adultery takes place.

Adultery is a sin against your *health*. We are in the midst of an epidemic of sexually transmitted diseases. Physically, multitudes of lives are being destroyed. AIDS is no longer just a disease found in the homosexual lifestyle. Other forms of social diseases are rapidly spreading. It is literally true that when you sleep with someone, you sleep with everyone with whom they have slept with. Adultery not only destroys physically but also emotionally. Ask anyone who has been involved in adultery about guilt. Ask the spouse about their hurt; ask the children and their children. It does not go away when the affair stops. The results of adultery continue.

When young people crawl out of the backseat after "going all the way," they have not gone all the way; they have just started. They have to face that person; they have to go home and face their parents. They have to live with what others say. They are affected in the present and the future when they have to explain to a future mate why they did not wait for them, or when telling their children why they should wait for marriage when they did not. Adultery is a sin against your health.

Adultery is a sin against your holy God. This perhaps should have been the first in the list because all sin is against God. When David faced his sin of adultery and cried out to God for forgiveness, he said in Psalm 51:4, "Against you, you only, have I sinned and done what is evil in your sight." He was not forgetting Bathsheba or her husband Uriah, but he knew that all sin is ultimately against God. No matter what extenuating circumstances you may use as an excuse, adultery flies in the face of God. He says, "Don't do it," and there is nothing that excuses it.

In counseling sessions, I have individuals say, "You know, I have prayed about this, and I know it is right." No, it is not; you don't have to pray about it. You already have the answer: "You shall not commit adultery." Years ago, I observed a couple for many weeks slip into the worship service just after we started singing, sit in the back row and slip out before the final prayer. Sometime later, it all came out; they were married to others, involved in an affair that broke up both homes, but told their families the affair was all right. They were going to church and felt peace about what they were doing. You cannot cover sin by wrapping it in the clothing of respectability. Adultery is a sin against God. All of God's rules are given so that life may be good. This commandment is no exception. The Jewish teachers called the violation of the Seventh Commandment "the great sin" because God used the husband and wife relationship to illustrate the relationship between Himself and His people.

Ministry in Marriage

There is also *ministry in marriage*. The marriage that God ordained is to be a relationship of giving and receiving. It is to be a partnership that brings mutual fulfillment. We are to minister to one another and to meet each other's needs. Husbands and wives minister to one another by loving one another. In the fifth chapter of Ephesians, the Apostle Paul discusses the relationship of the husband and wife. The well-quoted passage in Ephesians 5:22 says, "Wives, submit yourselves to your own husbands as you do to the Lord." However, the verse before says, "Submit to one another out of reverence for Christ." We must take it all. There is to be a mutual submission in love, one to another. This is God's plan.

Loving One Another

We are to *love one another*, emotionally. The Song of Solomon is a beautiful description of the emotion of love expressed between a husband and wife. I am not going to argue as some behavioral scientists do that we do not fall in love. However, the first emotion of love is not enough. We must continue to grow in love. I often hear, "Well, I just don't love him/her anymore." My answer is, "Start acting like you do; start doing the things you did when you first fell in love; start growing back in love." James Dobson says, "Love is a choice and it is. 'I don't love them anymore' is not a sufficient reason for breaking up a home. God is love and the God of love is the God of the home, and He is fully able to rekindle the spark of love that has burned low."

One way the emotion of love is shown is by the physical expression of love. In 1 Corinthians 7:5, the Apostle Paul tells married couples that they are not to deprive one another of sex. Only one exception is given and that is by mutual consent for a brief period while they devote themselves more fully to prayer. Sex within God's ordained parameters is good. In any other way, it is not good.

Listening to One Another

Furthermore, husbands and wives minister to each other by *listening to one another.* The book "Men are From Mars, Women are from Venus" touches upon something we need to understand. Men and women do not always "speak the same language." A friend of mine tells of the first year of their marriage being filled with some tough times. She would say to him, "Do you want to go to the movies tonight, or do you want to go out with some other couple and eat?" He would reply, "I don't care what we do." After about a year, she asked, "Why don't you ever want to do what I want to do?" He was perplexed, "I always want to do what you want to do." She replied, "Then why do you always say you don't care to do it?" She was hearing him say, "I don't care to do what you are asking me to do." He was saying, "It is okay with me if we do what you want to do." A limerick says, "To keep love brimming in the loving cup; when you're wrong admit it, when you're right shut up!"

Lifting One Another

We also minister to our spouse by *lifting them up.* There is no place for cutting each other down. So often in public, you will hear a husband or wife make some "put down" remark at the other's expense. If we love our spouse as Christ loved the church, we will build them up, not tear them down. Marriage is not, as often stated, a fifty-fifty proposition. It is a one hundred percent commitment on both parts. We need to learn to receive by giving instead of demanding. Lifting up one another ministers to the spouse's heart as well as to the ego. This is an important ministry of marriage.

What if you have already broken the Seventh Commandment? What if your spouse has? Adultery is not the unpardonable sin. You need to know that there is forgiveness. First John 1:9 says, "If we confess our sin, He is faithful and just to forgive us our sin and to cleanse us from all unrighteousness." There is forgiveness; there is restoration. We are not disqualified from God using us. There is forgiveness; however, there is also fallout. David provides a perfect example. He was restored but there was a price to be paid. His example before his children led them to similar behavior. It isn't easy to rebuild trust, but it can be done. It takes both parties in the marriage. It takes the submission of your wills to God's will and then you can experience His healing. Don't carry the burden of past sin. Confess it, and experience God's forgiveness.

In the book "Laws of the Heart," there are six practical suggestions for protecting your marriage. First, if you are not already married, decide that you will marry another Christian. Second, center your life on Jesus Christ and devote yourself to His word. Third, carefully follow every biblical guideline for improving your marriage. Fourth, make your spouse a priority. Fifth, meet your partner's sexual needs so completely that he or she will have no need to look elsewhere. Six, avoid relationships that might tempt you to commit adultery (Hybels 77–78). A healthy relationship with one another begins with a healthy relationship with God.

9.

◦〜◦

RESISTING THE
RIP-OFF

THE EIGHTH COMMANDMENT

You shall not steal.

Exodus 20:15

Without even realizing it, you are affected by the Eighth Commandment. You drive an automobile that is parked in a parking lot that you instinctively locked as you left. What does that have to do with the Eighth Commandment? When you leave your house, do you lock the doors and even set a security system if you have one? Does this have anything to do with the Eighth Commandment? The breaking of this commandment plays a large part in our daily lives. The possibility of losing our personal belongings or property to someone, who takes that which does not belong to them, affects all our lives seven days a week. "You shall not steal" touches us every day.

Stated in a positive manner, this commandment means that every individual has the divine right to own personal or private property. Thus far, we have seen that we have no right to take someone's life or wife. We have no reason or right to "rip off" people by taking their personal property or possessions. A closer look at the Eighth Commandment reveals the philosophy of a thief, the psychology of a thief, the perversion of a thief, and the pardon of a thief.

The Philosophy of a Thief

First, the *philosophy of the thief* shows that which lies at the foundation of one that steals. What is the thief's philosophy of life? What drives a person to develop an attitude that says, "I want and maybe even deserve something for nothing." This something-for-nothing attitude affects everything from the price we pay for a gallon of milk to our personal property taxes. With that kind of personal value system, a person can rationalize their way of thinking into believing that taking that which does not rightly belong to them is okay, as long as they don't get caught.

Comedian Joe E. Lewis once gave this definition of a thief: "One who just has a habit of finding things before people lose them!" A more serious definition would be: taking anything that rightly belongs to someone else, to take it secretly or by force (McGee 132).

The Right of Ownership

The philosophy of the thief conflicts directly with certain rights that each one of us has. It conflicts with *the right of ownership*. Psalm 24:1 tells us, "The earth is the Lord's and everything in it." True ownership belongs to God. However, He has given us the right of temporary ownership of things. Throughout the scriptures, we find teachings that establish this right of ownership. The philosophy of a thief taking that which is not his deprives us of that right. It is the philosophy that says, "What's yours is mine, and I'll take it. I don't care how much it means to you—if I want it, I'll get it if I can."

The Responsibility of Stewardship

The philosophy of the thief conflicts with the *responsibility of stewardship*. As temporary owners of God's creation, we are responsible for being good stewards of it. That which I have, I am responsible for. I am to manage it so that it produces the best for the true owner. My wife was born and reared on a farm, homesteaded by her grandfather. When he died, it passed into the possession of one of her uncles. However, her father lived on the farm and farmed it. At the end of each growing season, he was responsible to pay the true owner a share. That is where we get the term "sharecropper." In a sense, that is what we are for God. The thief, disregarding his responsibility of stewardship, sets out to rob us of our privilege of ownership and stewardship.

The Requirements of Workmanship

The philosophy of the thief conflicts with the requirements of workmanship. We are given the right of ownership and the proper way to obtain it. In the words of the television commercial, the old-fashioned way is to "earn it." There are honest ways to get what someone else has, work for it, or pay for it. Because a thief's philosophy is that of wanting something for nothing, someone else will always be on the losing side of this philosophy. However, the philosophy of the thief is the philosophy of the loser.

The Psychology of the Thief

The *psychology of the thief* is indeed interesting. The Bible gives us examples of people with "sticky fingers," people caught in the act of stealing. One of the most notable examples of this is a man by the name of Achan, whose thievery caused a devastating defeat of Israel's army at the town of Ai. God told the Israelites not to take any of the spoils of the pagan army in the battle of Jericho. They were ordered not to plunder and pillage their enemies' things. Yet, Achan disobeyed God's direct order, and his disobedience was found out. This one man's sin affected the entire nation of Israel and almost caused Israel to lose the Promised Land.

In Joshua 7:21, we find a perfect description of the psychology of a thief. When finally caught, Achan said, "When I saw in the plunder a beautiful robe from Babylonia, two hundred shekels of silver and a wedge of gold weighing fifty shekels, I coveted them and took them. They are hidden in the ground inside my tent, with the silver underneath." There was a threefold process going on inside Achan's head and heart.

First, there is the process of looking with the eyes. He said, "I saw." Stealing begins with a look. Achan saw some things he wanted and lost sight of God. When we see that which is forbidden, we oftentimes cannot help the first glimpse. However, it is not the first look that gets us into trouble but the second and the third look. The children's song says, "O, be careful little eyes what you see." The words of this little song are good advice, since that upon which we focus our attention oftentimes begins to take our focus off what was intended. This loss of focus can lead to a longing in the heart. The reclusive billionaire Howard Hughes was asked, "How much money does it take to make a man happy?" Hughes replied, "Just a little bit more." The longing heart is hard to satisfy.

Achan said, "I coveted." We will deal with the sin of coveting in the Tenth Commandment, but we cannot ignore covetousness as the reason for breaking the Eighth Commandment. One sees that which belongs to another, then begins to think about much how they would like to have it, and before you know it, a thief is born. Achan succumbed to the Devil's marketing plan. His lingering thoughts turned into longings, which were too strong to hold back.

The final step in Achan's journey from respectability to becoming a thief was completed with the lifting with his hands. In the words of one caught shoplifting, "I saw it and I lifted it." Achan said, "I took it." Achan discovered that taking something for nothing leads to losing everything. It was true then and is true today.

The Perversions of the Thief

The philosophy of the thief and the psychology of the thief lead to the *perversions of the thief.* Stealing takes many forms. First, there is what society calls the "common thief." We call them petty thieves, shoplifters, hijackers, hold-up men, burglars, robbers and many other such terms. These are the people that we read about everyday in the newspaper and hear about on the news. These are the ones against whom we lock our houses and cars to protect. It is alarming to read the statistics on how much is lost each year to the common thief. It is even more alarming to read the figures on the ages at which such behavior is beginning and the attitudes of children about stealing. A fourteen-year-old on a talk show looked at the host and said, "Why shouldn't I take it if they are stupid enough to allow it?" God said, "You shall not steal." End of discussion. Don't do it, because God said it is wrong.

Another type of thief is called the "camouflaged thief." The media calls him the "white collar" criminal. This title is a polite way to make this form of stealing seem more sophisticated and a step above the common thief. The shrewd operator develops slick sales pitch and writes the contract to his own unfair advantage. Another alters his expense account reports or cheats on his income tax.

Yet other forms of thievery are very much evident in our society. Take for example the one who steals through deception. A grocer may add weight to his scales. A car dealer may sell a car with very low mileage, when in fact the speedometer has been turned back. Another type of thief is the long-term borrower. This is the person who borrows something and then conveniently forgets to return the item and keeps it for his own (Hybels 89).

In his book "Playing by the Rules," Stuart Briscoe tells of visiting with the pollster, George Gallup. In the discussion, Gallup said that although religion has grown in popularity in our country, with church attendance, Bible reading, and other religious behaviors increasing, morality actually had declined. When Gallup did a test in conjunction with "The Wall Street Journal" asking questions about expense accounts, income taxes, and such, the polling group noted that a high percentage did not regard cheating on these items as stealing. Even more surprising, this attitude was present whether or not the people who were polled went to church. From the facts, George Gallup concluded that many of those who claim an interest in religion do not let religion affect their personal concept of morality in behavior (Briscoe 131).

An individual wrote to the Internal Revenue Service and said, "My conscience is bothering me. I owe you money that I have not paid. Here is a check for $100. P.S., if I still can't sleep, I will send you the rest of it!" Before we can experience revival in our land, we must understand that while the world may speak of "white-collar" crime, to God this form of stealing is as black and ugly as the crime of the common thief. Stealing is stealing, and God says, "Don't do it."

Then, there is the "church thief." In 1972, Paul Harvey reported on his noon news broadcast, the story of the thief who walked into a church on Sunday evening with a rifle and demanded all the money and jewelry from those in the congregation. That evening, my wife and daughter were in the congregation of the Hamlin Memorial Baptist Church, Springfield, Missouri. Of all times to be sick with the flu, I was home sick in bed. My wife gave an "offering" that evening. In fact, she put in all her money. When I asked why she had put it all in since he couldn't see her from where he stood, she had a great answer, "Because he had a gun!"

Stealing happens in different forms every Sunday. It has been going on for years. In Malachi 3, the prophet asked, "Will a man rob God?" It happened then, and it will happen today. Malachi said that we rob God when we fail to give our tithes and offerings. This is a very common way in which we break the Eighth Commandment. The tithe is not ours. Remember the principle of the right of ownership and stewardship. God is the owner of all things. We are the stewards of that with which He has blessed us. Just as the sharecropper owes a percentage of the crop to the owner for the use of the land, so we have been assessed the tithe as our requirement.

The tithe is not a gift to God. It is a requirement, and to fail to pay this obligation is to steal from God.

We are under grace and not under law; however, that does not mean that tithing has been eliminated from God's requirements. In fact, how can we consider doing less under grace than was expected under the law. The church thief steals in other ways. He steals when he neglects to give his family the time and leadership they need. He steals when he fails to give of his time to the church. The church needs you in areas of service.

The Pardon of a Thief

Lastly, we come to the pardon of a thief. Something must be done to stop this epidemic of thievery in our land. Like all other positive aspects, this needs to begin at the "house of the Lord." It must start with the people of God. We must recognize that Satan comes to steal. He is a master thief, and he is not interested in stealing money or possessions. He wants to steal your soul. If you do not know Jesus personally, Satan wants to ensure that you never come to know Him. He would steal your soul. If it is too late for that, if you have accepted Christ into your life, then he wants to steal away your salvation. Not the possession of it, for he cannot, but he wants to steal away the joy of our salvation. He also wants to steal away your service to the Savior.

Luke 8:11–12 tells us about Satan when it says, "Some people are like seed along the path, where the Word is sown. As soon as they hear it, Satan comes and takes away the Word that was sown in them."

While Satan comes to steal, the Son of God comes to save. On Mount Sinai, God laid down the law. On Mount Calvary, the Son of God laid down his life. He came to fulfill the law in every way. It is amazing that Jesus was crucified between two thieves. Between these two thieves, representing the sinfulness of man, our sinless Lord and Savior died. Before Jesus died for our sins, one thief reached out in faith and Jesus said to him, "Today you will be with me in paradise" (Luke 23:43).

Yes, there is hope for the thief. Because of the cross there is hope for the person:

Who profanes the name of God,

Who has made idols of the heart and home,

Who has dishonored parents,

Who has committed adultery,

Who has not remembered the Sabbath

And who has stolen.

We can find forgiveness in Christ. As He comes to reside in us, He will change our hearts. He will give us a new heart. The scripture says, "He who has been stealing must steal no longer, but must work, doing something useful with his own hands, that he may have something to share with those in need" (Ephesians 4:28). Stop doing that which is wrong and start doing that which is right. An internal change must take place and there must be an outward manifestation of this change. "God wants us to do more than take our hand out of the cookie jar. He wants us to bake cookies, not only for ourselves, but to have enough to be able to give some away" (Peel 189–190).

10.

❧

RINGING TRUE IN ALL YOU DO

THE NINTH COMMANDMENT

You shall not give false testimony against your neighbor.

Exodus 20:16

Our newspapers and broadcast news indicate that "truth-decay" has slowly but surely eroded our moral foundations. The moral foundation of America still appears sound, but like a building's foundation that has harbored a hungry horde of termites for a generation, our moral foundation is spiritually and structurally weakened. It seems that "truth" is bought and sold at the price of the highest paid legal dream-team or with the help of the best "spin doctors" in the public domain.

The Ninth Commandment is God's "gag-order" on bearing false witness against another. If truth came in a neatly wrapped package, it would have "Handle with Care" stamped all over it. Today, with God Almighty as our Judge and with His Word as our Witness, we are going to call truth to take the stand. Jesus said, "Then you will know the truth, and the truth will set you free" (John 8:32). As we examine the commandment, "You shall not give false testimony against your neighbor," we are going to allow the Bible to reveal to us the evidence that will stand the test of time.

There is a genealogy of the *falsehood family*. The movie "Twister" vividly illustrated the terrible damage a tornado can do. However, the movie was fiction. Real tornadoes have been reported in the news and we have seen film of communities destroyed by a twister in a short span of time. In the very beginning of creation, we find that the devil came into the Garden of Eden as the twister of truth. In a short amount of time, a paradise became a poisoned playground because of the devil and his deceptions. The witness of the Word reveals to us the father of lies.

The Father of Lies

In Genesis 3:1–7, we read of the *father of lies* introducing God's highest creation to the lie:

> Now the serpent was more crafty than any of the wild animals the Lord God had made. He said to the woman, "Did God really say, 'You must not eat from any tree in the garden'?" The woman said to the serpent, "We may eat fruit from the trees in the garden, but God did say, 'You must not eat from the tree that is in the middle of the garden, and you must not touch it, or you will die'." "You will not surely die," the serpent said to the woman. "For God knows that when you eat of it your eyes will be opened, and you will be like God, knowing good and evil." When the woman saw the fruit of the tree was good for food and pleasing to the eye, and also desirable for gaining wisdom, she took some and ate it. She also gave some to her husband, who was with her, and he ate it. Then the eyes of both of them were opened, and they realized they were naked; so they sewed fig leaves together and made coverings for themselves.

The devil questioned God's goodness and justice, and he made promises he would not keep. In trying to live this lie, Adam and Eve tried to hide from God. Built into the genetic code of every lie is rebellion against a Holy God. Lying is sinful because God is true. John 8:44 says, "You belong to your father, the devil, and you want to carry out your father's desire. He was a murderer from the beginning, not holding to the truth, for there is no truth in him. When he lies, he speaks his native language, for he is a liar and the father of lies." The Word has given us a witness. The devil is the father of all lies and the proud father of a very dysfunctional family of lies. We can trace every lie back to him. He has not repented nor changed his ways. He has only become cleverer in his twisting of the truth.

First Family of Lies

From the father of lies comes the *first family of lies*. Genesis 2:25 tells us that "Adam and his wife were both naked, and they felt no shame." Their relationship was built on absolute truth and openness. They had absolutely nothing to hide from each other or God. When they accepted the devil's fatal falsehood, they immediately felt the pain and void of being so very far from God's personal presence. They had been duped. They immediately planned a "cover-up." They invented the blame game. As one writer puts it, "down through the generations the lie has been perpetuated. If I can hide, then I am safe" (Peel 206).

First Born of Lies

The first family of lies produced the *first born of lies*. His name was Cain, and we find him lying to God in Genesis 4:9 when God asked him where his brother was. He said, "I don't know." Then Cain asked God a smart-mouthed question, "Am I my brother's keeper?" The lying tongue became the insolent tongue. In the very first human relationships, we see that it is wrong to bear false witness in the community of life and in the court of law. Truth is essential if life is to be lived in harmony with God and with one another.

Today, we continue to live with the results of the guile of the falsehood family. The fraternity of falsehoods with all their strange friends and fellows have learned to shade the truth in many creative ways. In the "Library of Liars," we find what a friend calls a "laundry list of lying gibberish." The very first lie was one of heresy, a most difficult lie to deal with because it has elements that resemble the truth. Wrapping elements of the truth of God in the overall words of a lie, Satan deceived Adam and Eve. Today, Satan continues to speak heresy through those who have been deceived or willfully spread false teachings for personal gain. Many are being robbed of the truth about God, His purpose, His plan for their lives, His place of eternal abode because they have fallen victim to heresy spawned by the father of lies. One of the great heresies of our day is the lie that there is no absolute truth, that truth is relative. We have been deceived by the teaching of "situational ethics," which tells us that the circumstances determine the truth.

Closely resembling heresy is the sin of hearsay. "They said" or "some have said" are words we hear all the time. The courts will not accept hearsay evidence, but it is repeated so freely by so many that this type of evidence is often accepted as truth without question. Leviticus 19:16 says, "Do not go about spreading slander among your people." First Timothy 5:13 speaks of those who "get into the habit of being idle and going about from house to house. And not only do they become idlers, but also busybodies who talk nonsense, saying things they ought not to." The next time you hear, "They say"; you need to ask, "Who is the 'they' who say what you say they say?" You need to ask, "Is it alright if I use your name when I repeat this?" Or ask, "Who are 'they,' because I would really like to know so that I can check out the truth of this?" Because of the tremendous amount of damage done by a lie, it is a small wonder that Proverbs 6 tells us that God hates seven things, and two of the seven are about lies, "a lying tongue" and "a false witness who pours out lies" (Proverbs 6:17–19). In Proverbs 26:20 we read, "Without wood a fire goes out; without gossip a quarrel dies down."

Holy Lies

Holy lies are things said in the name of religion and this type of lie hurts so very deeply. The book of Acts gives us the story of a husband and wife team of liars named Ananias and Sapphira. They conspired together to lie to God and the church that they might be looked up to as "super saints." Their plan backfired and led to their destruction. Their actions hurt others greatly. When people, in the name of God, speak that which is untrue, the kingdom of God suffers. The Psalmist, in Psalm 52:2, tells us that "Lies are like a sharp razor... they cut." Anyone who has been in church work for any period of time has seen firsthand the hurt wrought by a careless tongue. James warns us, "but no human being can tame the tongue. It is a restless evil, full of deadly poison" (James 3:8).

One of the most difficult lies to deal with is that of the half-truth. It is harder to stop the half-truth than a whole lie. The element of truth in the lie makes it difficult to know where the truth ends, and the lie begins. However, it is important to note that there is a difference in telling a half-truth and telling everything you know about the truth. There are those who think they have to give all the details, including details that may be hurtful. In fact, some individuals delight in giving all the "juicy" details and saying, "Well, you know, I just have to tell the truth." Yes, you do, but you should be sure that everything you tell needs to be told.

Homicidal Lies

Homicidal lies or character assassination are particularly harmful. To slander another's reputation is to rob them of a most prized possession. So hurtful is this type of falsehood, that God says in Psalm 101:5, "Whoever slanders their neighbor in secret, I will put him to silence." It is difficult to survive a vicious "drive-by shooting off of the mouth." We must be particularly careful because we can slander someone without really saying anything untrue. This often occurs by insinuation, a seemingly innocent question, a shrug, or silence, when a word of defense or clarification is needed. Jesus was a victim of this type of lie. "We are not illegitimate children," was a statement from Jesus' enemies in John 8:41. The statement was true, they were not; but the implication was that Jesus was illegitimate and this statement from his enemies was designed to defame Jesus' character.

There is a story of a first mate on a sailing ship who was found drunk on his watch. He had an unblemished record until this incident. He begged the captain not to write up this offense in his daily log. However, the captain would not listen and entered into his log, "The first mate was drunk today." The first mate smarted from this tarnishing of his record and one day saw his chance for revenge, when he was responsible for entering his report into the log. He simply wrote, "The captain was sober today."

There is no coloring the truth in God's eyes. Harmless lies are the little things that we justify by saying, "it's just a little white lie." Saying things like, "What a lovely outfit you have on," when you were thinking *what terrible taste you have.* Or telling the preacher, "Great sermon this morning," when you slept through it. God doesn't separate lies into black or white, big or little; He just says, "Tell the truth...don't lie."

Truth acts as a tongue-suppressor. It is too bad that people cannot stick with the truth. Often, the liar is caught by the truth because he does not have enough memory chips to keep up with his lies. The Father of truth does not leave those who succumb to the father of lies without hope. There is grace for the falsehood family. The God of grace shows grace to those in need of grace because of the sin of lying.

The Father of truth knows that all men are liars. Psalm 116:11 says it just that way. Inherent in the sinful nature of mankind is the propensity for lying. It begins in infancy. Notice the baby, who is crying at the top of his or her voice, screaming, as if something is wrong. Then, notice the quick smile that comes to be baby's face, when some attention is given to him.

Nothing was really wrong with the child; the child had learned to act as if something was wrong in order to receive attention.

The Father of truth knows that the liar can be forgiven but the lie lives on. Few things are more difficult to undo than the hurt that results from a lie. The story is told of a woman, who came to her pastor and confessed the sin of gossip. She wanted to be free from her guilt. He helped her to understand that God forgives all sin, as we are told in 1 John 1:9, "If we confess our sin, he is faithful and just and will forgive us our sin and cleanse us from all unrighteousness." Then the pastor asked the woman to do a very strange thing. He asked her to go to the nearby seashore and fill a sack with sand and bring it back to him. When she returned with the sack of sand, he asked her to go to an open window and pour the sand out into the wind. Then he asked her to go outside and pick up the sand. "That is impossible," replied the woman. "So," the pastor said, "It is equally impossible for you to ever retract all your hurtful words." That is why it is so important that we remember the words of Ephesians 4:25, "Therefore each of you must put off falsehood and speak truthfully to your neighbor."

The Father of truth knows that the believer faces a constant accuser. We are constantly being confronted with opportunities where we are tempted to speak an untruth. It is a part of the evil one's daily onslaught against us. Because the Father knows this, He gives us directions to confront the temptation to speak and live in a way that is untrue. In 1 John 2:1 we are told, "But if anybody does sin, we have an advocate with the Father—Jesus Christ, the Righteous One." He knows who can save us. "For the law was given through Moses; grace and truth came through Jesus Christ" (John 1:17). The father of lies has been defeated by the Father of truth through the atoning work at Calvary. Truth is available to each of us through the Lord Jesus. By grace we can have victory over that which is untrue.

For each negative in the Ten Commandments, there is a corresponding positive. The positive in the Ninth Commandment says, "You shall speak and live that which is true." Ephesians 4:15 tells us to speak truth in love. Matthew 12:37 says, "For by your words you will be acquitted, and by our words you will be condemned." Our words give evidence of who we are and whose we are. To be able to speak truth, we must know truth, and to know truth, we must know Him, who is truth. In John 14:6, Jesus says, "I am...the truth." To know truth, we must know Him. He is the starting point of truth.

11.

∽

RIDING HERD ON YOUR DESIRES

THE TENTH COMMANDMENT

You shall not covet your neighbor's house. You shall not covet your neighbor's wife, or his male or female servant, his ox or donkey, or anything that belongs to your neighbor.

Exodus 20:17

The *desire to acquire* is God given. In fact, we are instructed to desire certain things. Paul tells us to eagerly desire spiritual gifts. The *need to succeed* is also God given. Second Timothy 2:15 says, "Do your best to present yourself to God as one approved, a worker who does not need to be ashamed and who correctly handles the word of truth." The *juice to produce* is also God given. Adrenalin pumps and creative juices flow because God built them into our system.

All of these are part of what it means to be created in the likeness and image of God.

However, these same gifts from God, which are so essential to successfully living life to the fullest, are equally destructive. The desire to acquire, when carried to its covetous extreme, caused Ahab to kill his neighbor, Naboth, for his vineyard. This same desire to acquire caused David to take his neighbor's wife and kill her husband. It caused local officials to accept bribes and be forced to resign in disgrace. It causes many to spend money far beyond their means, mortgaging the future for the present.

The need to succeed, when carried to its covetous extreme, caused James and John to enlist the help of their mother in attempting to persuade Jesus to give them a favored position in the heavenly kingdom. The need to succeed has enticed world class athletes to enhance their chances of winning by taking illegal drugs. It has caused racing teams to soup up their engines beyond the legal limits. The need to succeed has caused many of God's children to neglect things that they might have succeeded in that were temporal.

The juice to produce, when carried to its covetous extreme, caused Simon, the sorcerer, to try to buy the gift of miracles. He wanted to produce the gift of the Holy Spirit in the lives of others, a worthy goal. However, he wanted to produce this gift by his efforts, rather than by his commitment. The juice to produce also caused Simon Peter to grab a sword and cut off the ear of one of the high priest's servants. It also causes busy families to sacrifice home and family for success in their chosen field of work. At times, it causes God's people to do "godly things" in their own power without considering God's will.

The first nine commandments deal with sins of actions, sins that are outwardly expressed. The violation of the first nine commandments is the acting out of the inner sin of covetousness; the invisible sins of the mind become visible in our conduct. The Tenth Commandment is one of the most difficult with which to deal, as it brings us to focus upon that which is inward, or sins of attitude. The first nine commandments speak of that which we do; the Tenth Commandment speaks of that which we think. Remember the words of Proverbs 23:7, "For as he thinks in his heart, so is he" (NKJV). The invisible sins of the mind become visible in our conduct.

The Tenth Commandment lists a number of desires

that the wise person must realize can touch his life with death and destruction at any moment. Listen to what this commandment says in its entirety: "You shall not covet your neighbor's house. You shall not covet your neighbor's wife, or his male or female servant, his ox or donkey, or anything that belongs to your neighbor" (Exodus 20:17).

Crisis of Identity

Looking closely at this scripture will cause us to realize that a person who is consumed with coveting is actually experiencing a *crisis of identity.* One writer has stated that this section of the Ten Commandments is intensely personal because covetousness takes place in the quiet recesses of the human heart (McClanahan 80).

I do not know about you, but I find myself wishing that God had stopped with the Ninth Commandment. I feel better when I look at things than when I grapple with things I think. I can hide my thoughts from you, but I cannot hide them from myself! Coveting is the most subtle and deceitful of all the sins listed in God's ledger of laws.

Dissatisfaction with God's Blessings

When you look at the Tenth Commandment in detail, you find that the covetous person is *dissatisfied with God's blessings.* Their neighbor's house is the first forbidden item that God warns against coveting. It is easy to become dissatisfied with our living quarters. In Luke 12, we find the parable of the man Jesus called the rich fool. This man decided to tear down his barns and build bigger ones. Today, we rarely do this; we just sell our house and buy or build a bigger one in a more affluent neighborhood. According to one Christian counselor, women tend to find their identity in their home, while men find it more in the workplace. If you are not careful, you can become dissatisfied with where you are.

Dissatisfaction with our Spouse

God also warns us against becoming *dissatisfied with our spouse.* "You shall not covet your neighbor's [spouse]," we are told. The Seventh Commandment warns against the sin of adultery. Mark 7:21–23 says, "For it is from within, out of a person's heart, that evil thoughts come—sexual immorality, theft, murder, adultery, greed...All these evils come from inside and defile a person." The Living Bible translation replaces the word "greed" with "wanting what belongs to others." That is coveting. It is from the sin of coveting that the sin of leaving one's spouse and becoming involved with another person comes.

Dissatisfaction with our Laborers

This commandment also speaks of becoming *dissatisfied with our laborers.* Most of us do not have servants, but many of us are responsible for filling positions in our company. It is easy to covet someone else's employees. At a luncheon, a church deacon was discussing the retirement of the pastor. He began talking about one of the staff members of the church I pastored as a replacement. I listened for a few moments and then, in my best Clint Eastwood, Dirty Harry voice said, "Don't even think about it!"

The other side of this coin is to covet the job someone else has; to lose the joy of our work because "the grass is greener on the other side of the fence." This was so vividly illustrated as I looked out the window of my former home. We lived on twenty acres and had a few head of cattle. My cattle and those of my neighbor had come together along the fence. For almost a quarter of a mile, the cattle were grazing with their heads through the fence, straining as afar as they could to eat the grass on the other side of the fence.

Often, coveting is the "killer of contentment," robbing us of the joy that God has given us. Legal belongings, those described in the commandment as "your neighbors ox and donkey, or anything that belongs to him," are off limits. Our neighbor has a right to what belongs to him; we have a right to that which is ours. We have a right to acquire more, but there is a way to do it that does not involve coveting. The person who is trying to "keep up with the Joneses" has a hard time maintaining a prayer life, a devotional life, or a life committed to God. They suffer from a real crisis identity. They want the life and lives of others instead of the life they have in Christ.

Conspiracy of Injury

Not only is the covetous person experiencing a crisis of identity, but he also is experiencing a *conspiracy of injury.* William Barclay wrote, "to covet is not merely to desire something which one does not possess; it is to desire something which one has no right to possess" (Barclay 14). Covetousness, when left unchecked, may eventually lead to someone getting hurt. Someone will end up a loser. Someone will lose a house, a home, a mother, a father, a living and lifestyle, an inheritance, a future. This is the conspiracy of injury because that is exactly the way the devil works. It starts out small and seemingly innocent and then grows. Psalm 1:1 depicts the blessed man as one "who does not walk in step with the wicked or stand in the way of sinners take or sit in the company of mockers." This is how the conspiracy is presented. First, the sinful person walks among the enemy; then, he stands with them until he finally sits among them as one of them.

In riding herd on our desires, we need to realize the process that Satan uses. One thought enters our mind; we allow it to dwell there until the thought expands. You see an automobile and like it. You continue to think about how you would like to have that automobile and the first thing you know you are figuring out a way to get it. The principle to remember is one thought becomes two thoughts. Before you know it, two thoughts become a way of seeing things. You become convinced that it is your right to have the automobile. You become convinced not only that you can have it, but also that it is God's will for you to have that car. The same thing happened in the Garden of Eden. Eve saw; she thought, and she decided that which she had believed needed to be changed.

Desire to Possess

The next step in the conspiracy is that the way of seeing things becomes a *desire to possess.* Remember the story of Aachan from the commandment on stealing. In Joshua 7 we hear him say, "I saw it...I coveted." That which he allowed himself to look at, he began to desire. Eve saw the fruit and it looked good; she wanted it. When left unchecked, a desire leads to a strong desire. One of the tragic stories in the life of David tells of his son who lusted after his sister and became obsessed with having her. Oftentimes one says, "It just grew until I could not get it out of my mind." The words of Micah 2:1 best express how this happens. "Woe to those who plan iniquity...because it is in their power to do it." A strong desire leads to certain actions. Achan said, "I saw it...I coveted it...I took it!" Many of us have looked back and said, "I cannot believe I did that." The scripture warns us that after desire has conceived, it gives birth to sin (James 1:15). It is true; strong desire leads to certain actions.

Actions often lead to habits and habits lead to strongholds in our life. This is a process, yet, it does not take long to fully develop. The devil would have us believe that just a little look does not hurt. Just thinking about it is all right; even desiring is not wrong. It is like the spider's web that lures the insect closer until it is trapped.

Case of Idolatry

The crisis of identity and the conspiracy of injury result in a *case of idolatry.* In breaking the Tenth Commandment, we see that sin spins full circle, back to the very First Commandment. In the First Commandment, God says, "You shall have no other gods before me." Covetousness will allow everything else to take the front seat in our lives. People, objects, leisure, wants, and wishes fill our minds and lives, everything except God. Paul tells us in Colossians 3:5, "Put to death, therefore, whatever belongs to our earthly nature: sexual immorality, impurity, lust, evil desires and greed, which is idolatry." In Ephesians 5:3 Paul says there is

166

not to be even a hint of sexual immorality or any kind of impurity or greed among God's people. For these to reign in our lives is for us to be guilty of breaking the First Commandment. We have made idols of them and they have become our gods.

Breaking the Tenth Commandment does two things: It captivates our minds and it sabotages our convictions (Hybels 112). In their book, "Where is Moses When We Need Him?," Bill and Kathy Peel stated it this way:

> *"The more I put in, the more I want—That's Greed. The more I want, the more I need— That's Emptiness. The more I need, the more I become obsessed—That's Slavery. We might add, the more we become enslaved, the less God is in control—That's idolatry."*

There is a story, purported to be true, of a man who asked to be buried in his gold Cadillac. As they were filling in the grave, one of the attendants was overheard to say, "Man, that's living!" We have allowed our priorities to get out of order. Idolatry has sprung from the seed of coveting, which clouds our thinking, until we do not see things clearly. We need to replace covetous-ness with contentment. Hebrews 13:5–6 says, "Keep your lives free from the love of money and be content with what you have."

As we have gone through the commandments, perhaps you have been feeling pretty good. You may have breezed along feeling that you were doing well in keeping the commandments, no stealing, no killing, no adultery. You may have even been feeling pretty good about your relationship with God. How well are you really doing? In Romans 7, Paul touches on this very thing. He was reared in a strict religious setting. Paul was educated to be a religious leader and lived an exemplary life. In fact, he indicates that he would not have come to the realization that he was a sinner, if it had not been for the Tenth Commandment, which brought him face to face with the fact that sin was alive in his life. Paul could not say that he had never covet-ed and when he realized it, he recognized that covet-ousness touched other areas of his life.

We need to be honest with ourselves and God. Thoughts may have turned into ways of seeing things; ways of seeing things into strong desire and strong desire into actions. You may be in danger of acting.

Some readers may already have allowed actions to become habits, strongholds in their lives. If so, deal with this and let God tear down the strongholds. Many of us need to admit what is in control in our lives. We need to be honest with God and allow Him to be what we covet, instead of the things of this world. Where are our priorities?

12.

∾

RELATING THE LAW TO LIFE

On one occasion an expert in the law stood up to test Jesus. "Teacher," he asked, "what must I do to inherit eternal life?" "What is written in the Law?" he replied. "How do you read it?" He answered, "'Love the Lord your God with all your heart and with all your soul and with all your strength and with all your mind' and, 'Love your neighbor as yourself.'" "You have answered correctly," Jesus replied. "Do this and you will live."

Luke 10:25–28

The giant letters on the billboard read "JUST DO IT." A graffiti artist had punctuated it with a somewhat misshapen question mark. He must have been in a questioning mood for farther down the road was a sign that read "JUST SAY NO." Again, there was the spray-painted question mark. It was a fair question. If he was going to just do it, he needed to know what it

171

was he was supposed to do. Before he could just say no, he must have an understanding of what it was he was saying "no" to. Both question marks were legitimate.

In studying the Law of God, the Ten Commandments stand before the Christian as giant billboards saying. "Just do it! Just say no!" If there is to be a revival in our land, the people of God are not only going to have to learn the Word of God, they are going to have to live the Law of God. When it says, "Just do it!" They must do it. When it says, "Just say no!" They must just say no. The words of Judges 17:6, "In those days Israel had no king; everyone did as they saw fit," can no longer be the rule of our land.

It is not enough that only twenty percent of Americans claim to talk with God. More than thirteen percent of Americans must come to accept all Ten Commandments as applicable today. Twenty percent of the church members cannot carry eighty percent of the load. One of the things that so often brought Jesus into conflict with the religious leaders of his day was His insistence upon making the Law of God practical. It was more than something to be learned and revered, it was something to be lived. So, when Jesus saw a crippled man, He healed him, even though it was the Sabbath. Jesus insisted that faith must be lived out.

On one occasion, Jesus found Himself facing a hostile group of teachers of the law and an interesting conversation took place. In Luke 10:25–28, we find Jesus telling these teachers how the law applied to their lives. The eleventh command is putting the other Ten Commandments into action. There is no value in a law if it is not kept. The law that says you must not kill is of no value to the family of a murder victim; their loved one is dead. The law was not obeyed. That the law says, "Thou shall not commit adultery," and it safeguards no family if it is ignored. The eleventh command tells us to put what we know into action, live what we have learned.

From the conversation between Jesus and the lawyer in Luke 10, there are three lessons we need to learn. Lesson number one is found in the word "Eternal." The question, "What must I do to inherit eternal life?" was a legitimate question. However, the "tester" did not have the purest of motives. It was his intent to elicit from Jesus an answer that would bring him into conflict with the Law. He was an expert in the Law and wanted to start a debate.

America, today, is filled with those who would tear down the faith rather than build it up. There are those who are looking for something with which to find fault. Religious debates rage. Denominations are making decisions that are causing schisms among their leadership and within their congregations. The church, today, does not need to be testing the Law of God; it needs to be living it.

In the Luke passage, the conversation turned around rather quickly. The one being tested quickly became the teacher. Jesus answered a question with a question. "What is written in the Law?" He establishes for us a principle for finding the answer to the problems of life. When you need an answer to the problems of life, go to the Word. When He speaks of the Law, Jesus is referring to the Old Testament Law, which was approximately 1,500 years old at the time, but still relevant. It is approximately 3,500 years old today and the Law is equally as viable for life today, as it was when it was given.

The second question is of extreme importance. "How do you read it?" In this context, Jesus is probably asking no more than for the lawyer to tell Him what the law said. There is something more there for you and me and may have been in the original asking. Not asking simply, "Do you know what the Word says?" The more important question is, "Do you understand what it means?" It is not enough to know the Word, which is eternal. If it is to have meaning in life, we must not only know the eternal Word, but also the Word must become internal.

The lawyer knew the answer in theory. He knew the Word. So, we hear the lawyer answer, "'Love the Lord your God with all your heart and with all your soul and with all your strength and with all your mind,' and 'Love your neighbor as yourself.'" The lawyer's answer is a direct quotation of the Shema, the passage which the people were instructed to learn, to teach to their children and write on the doorpost of their homes. Many of them carried it with them in a pouch called phylacteries, strapped around their forehead. It was everywhere. Found in Deuteronomy 6, it stopped with loving God with all your heart, soul, strength, and mind. The matter of loving your neighbor as yourself is from Leviticus 19:18. The lawyer showed he knew not only the Law but also the application of the Law.

The reading of the Law goes deeper. It is a heart matter. We are to love the Lord where we live. We are to love Him with our soul, our mind and our strength. This is what makes us who we are. This is what the essence of life truly is, to be totally enmeshed in loving God. Jesus did not mince any words with the lawyer when He spoke about his response. Jesus simply says, "You know what to do, now do it!" Earlier, the lawyer had answered in theory. He knew the words; he knew what to say, but Jesus' response indicates that the lawyer was not living what he taught. The lawyer had the Word of God in his head, but he did not have the God of the Word in his heart.

The same problem exists today. Churches are filled with those who know the Word of God but exhibit no walk with God. From the pulpit to the pew, there are those whose talk and walk are not the same. The Word eternal must become the Word internal, then it must become the Word lived externally. The lawyer knew this to be the case, which is why he added to the Shema the words about loving one's neighbor. However, when told to go and live what he professed, the lawyer attempted to evade responsibility for externalizing the Word by asking another question.

What's Yours is Mine, I'll take it

This time the question was, "Who is my neighbor?" Jesus responded with the beautiful story of the Good Samaritan. No story more profoundly sets forth the vertical and horizontal aspects of our walk with God. Three attitudes are found in this story. The first attitude is that of the thieves which says, *"What is yours is mine and I will take it."* The thieves saw a man with possessions and their only thought was "How can I get it for myself?" This story vividly portrays the Ten Commandments. The thieves broke the Tenth Commandment by coveting what the man possessed. They broke the First and Second Commandments by making material things their god. They broke the Eighth Commandment by taking what the man had by force, and had not the Samaritan rescued the victim, they would have broken the Sixth Commandment by taking the man's life. The outward conduct of the thieves showed their inner character.

What's Mine is Mine, I'll keep it

The second attitude was seen in the conduct of the religious leaders, the priests and the Levites, who came upon the scene after the robbery, saw the victim, and passed by without offering any help. Their attitude was *"What's mine is mine, and I will keep it."* How we treat each other shows what we are really like on the inside. It is not enough to talk the Christian talk. We must walk the Christian walk, as well. James warns in James chapter 2, when he speaks of the one who sees another in need and says, "Go in peace; keep warm and well fed" yet does nothing about it. In verse 17 he writes, "faith by itself, if it is not accompanied by action, is dead." The religious leaders showed by their external conduct that the eternal Word did not dwell in them. The church is often criticized for being more talk than action. It often gives the feeling that it does not care. Remember that the church is its people. We must be honest and ask, "What kind of message does our church send to the world around us?"

What's Mine is Yours, I'll Share it

The third attitude was the attitude of the Samaritan. Even though his people were enemies of the victim, the Samaritan practiced the philosophy of *"What is mine is yours, and I will share it."* He showed love to one, who perhaps would not have done the same for him had the roles been reversed. This was not an issue for the Samaritan. He was not responsible for the actions of others, only for his own actions. He went beyond the superficial. He got down to where theory and reality cross. It was "put up or shut up" time and he put up and beyond. The Samaritan not only took care of the victims' immediate need, he also took the man to a resting place, paid for his care, and promised to do more if needed when he came back. The Samaritan lived what he professed. He demonstrated the eleventh commandment in action.

Students of an abnormal psychology class were assembled for their final exam. As the students received the test, some groaned, some moaned in astonishment, others began immediately to write the answers. Others sat for a considerable period of time before lifting a pencil. Several students finished in less than one hour, while others were still laboring over the answers at the end of the two-hour allotted test period. Remarks from the students ranged from, "That was the most unfair test I have ever taken" to "That was a good test, it really showed whether we knew the material or not." The professor had simply written ten paragraphs describing ten different mental patients and asked for a diagnosis. Students, who could have defined every term in the textbook, had absolutely no idea how to make a diagnosis; they were lost. Grades on the exam ranged from zero to perfect scores. The difference in grades was due to whether you knew the definitions or whether you knew what the definitions meant.

When thinking of the Christian life, we must determine if we only know the words or if we live the words. There is a great difference. In John 13:34–35, Jesus said, "A new command I give you: Love one another. As I have loved you, so you must love one another. By this everyone will know that you are my disciples, if you love one another."

Our nation stands in need of revival. If revival is to come, it must come from the people of God. We must begin to live lives that point others to God. The church can no longer sit and play church; it must be the church Christ intended for it to be. We must become the standard by which life is judged. It must not be said that the world has become so "churchy" and the church so worldly, that one cannot tell where one ends and the other begins.

BIBLIOGRAPHY

Barclay, William. *The Ten Commandments for Today.* Harper Collins Publishers, 10 East 53rd Street, New York, New York 10022, 1983.

Briscoe, Stuart. *The Ten Commandments: Playing by the Rules.* Harold Shaw Publishers, Box 567, Wheaton, Illinois, 1993.

Davidman, Joy. *Smoke on the Mountain: An Interpretation of the Ten Commandments.* Westminster Press, Philadelphia, Pennsylvania, 1953.

Honeycutt, Roy L. *These Ten Words.* Broadman Press, Nashville, Tennessee, 1966.

Huffman, John A. Jr. *Liberating Limits: A Fresh Look at the Ten Commandments.* World Books Publisher, Waco, Texas, 1980.

Hughes, R. Kent. *Disciplines of Grace: God's Ten Words for a Vital Spiritual Life*. Crossways Books, Wheaton, Illinois, 1993.

Hybels, Bill. *Laws of the Heart: 10 Essentials of a Liberated Life*. Victor Books, Wheaton, Illinois, 1985.

Morgan, G. Campbell. *The Ten Commandments*. Fleming H. Revell Company, Chicago, Illinois, 1901.

Peel, Bill & Kathy. *Where is Moses When We Need Him?: Teaching Your Kids the Ten Values That Matter Most*. Broadman & Holman Publishers, Nashville, Tennessee, 1995.

Vines, Jerry. *Basic Bible Sermons on The Ten Commandments*. Broadman Press, 1992.